Sir Frederick Pollock

A First Book of Jurisprudence

for Students of the Common Law

Sir Frederick Pollock

A First Book of Jurisprudence
for Students of the Common Law

ISBN/EAN: 9783337314866

Printed in Europe, USA, Canada, Australia, Japan

Cover: Foto ©Suzi / pixelio.de

More available books at **www.hansebooks.com**

A FIRST BOOK

OF

JURISPRUDENCE

FOR STUDENTS OF THE COMMON LAW

BY

SIR FREDERICK POLLOCK, BART.

BARRISTER-AT-LAW

M.A., HON. LL.D. EDIN., DUBLIN AND HARVARD
CORPUS CHRISTI PROFESSOR OF JURISPRUDENCE IN THE UNIVERSITY OF OXFORD
LATE FELLOW OF TRINITY COLLEGE, CAMBRIDGE
CORRESPONDING MEMBER OF THE INSTITUTE OF FRANCE

London
MACMILLAN AND CO., LTD.
NEW YORK: THE MACMILLAN CO.
1896

PREFACE

This book is not intended to lay out a general system of the philosophy of law, nor to give a classified view of the whole contents of any legal system, and it does not profess to compete with the many works which have aimed at one or both of those objects. It is addressed to readers who have laid the foundation of a liberal education and are beginning the special study of law. Such a reader finds, in the new literature he has to master, a number of leading conceptions and distinctions which are assumed to be familiar, and are so to lawyers, but which, for that very reason, are not often expressly stated, still less often discussed, and hardly ever explained. He has not only to discover for himself, often with much bewilderment, the actual contents of legal terms, but to realise the legal point of view and the legal habit of mind. Law seems to the layman, at first sight, to make much of trifles and to disregard greater matters. Again, some speculative problems are capable of giving much trouble in the actual practice and administration of the law, while others are seldom or never heard of in court; and it is hard for the layman or the novice to distinguish the two kinds. In this as in other sciences every one must make his way through the stage of confusion and illusion in his own fashion. But, though it is his own work which no one else can do for him, it is possible for those who have passed beyond that adventure to be ready with a helping hand and a warning voice.

In the first part of this book I have tried to set forth, in language intelligible to scholars who are not yet lawyers, so much of the general ideas underlying legal discussions as appeared needful for the removal of the most pressing difficulties. Not much will be found about constitutional or criminal law; not because I underrate their actual importance, but because they do not, as a rule, so much require this kind of explanation, and their exceptional problems, when they do occur, are too hard for novices, and are best left for a riper stage. Quotation and criticism of other modern writers' opinions have been, with rare exceptions, purposely avoided as useless and distracting to those for whom I mainly write. Any detailed acknowledgment of my obligations will therefore not be expected. Among the authors of past generations I owe most, so far as I can judge, to Savigny; among recent and living ones to Maine, Ihering, and my friend Mr. Justice Holmes of Massachusetts. Learned readers and advanced students will easily see that the philosophy of the English or "analytical" school is not mine; nevertheless I have learned much from Hobbes, and hold acquaintance with his work at first hand indispensable for all English-speaking men who give any serious consideration to the theoretical part of either politics or law. It may be that I love Hobbes a little too well to be perfectly just to his successors, who, to my thinking, have often got more praise than they deserved for repeating Hobbes's ideas in clumsier and really less exact words. But, as I am not undertaking a critical estimate, this is but a matter of personal taste, and of no importance to the reader.

While I have endeavoured to be as clear as possible, I have not attempted to make fundamental and difficult problems look easy. The cheap facility that comes of gliding over hard

practical art can really be taught; one man can only help another to learn; but it is common experience that such help will often save a great deal of trouble. Certainly no man ever learned to shoot by being lectured on the construction of a rifle, and yet such lectures are a regular part of musketry instruction. So far as I know, the experiment has never been made, in the case in hand, for the same purpose or in any very similar manner, though different parts of the subject have been touched upon by several writers, both English and American, on legal studies and literature, and notably by Kent. Possibly a connected account of the sources and authorities of English law, as they have come to be in modern practice, may be of interest to some of the Continental scholars, especially Frenchmen, who of late years have brought admirable industry and intelligence to bear on our methods of conducting both political and judicial affairs. But I have written, in the first place, for our own learners of the Common Law on both sides of the ocean, and my work stands to be judged by their proof in using it. If they find it useful I shall be well content, even more content than if I should perchance convince a mature philosopher or economist that the science of law has some right to exist.

places can only be found a dear bargain in the end. Sometimes I have allowed myself to devote a few sentences or even a paragraph to readers who have to some extent mastered the language and methods of philosophy. This, I hope, will not be unwelcome to such as have taken honour degrees in classics, especially in the Oxford School of *Literae Humaniores.*

The second part of the book aims at an end not really dissimilar in kind, but it is more practical and more exclusively addressed to students of the Common Law, the system according to which justice is administered in almost every part of the English-speaking world except Scotland and (if that be a real exception) Louisiana. Like the Roman law, that system is embodied in a special and technical literature governed by its own authoritative conventions, accessible only through its own apparatus of reference, and available for any practical purpose only on condition of understanding its peculiar methods. The use of law-books and the appreciation of legal authorities can be fully learned only by assiduous practice; but here, again, it has long seemed to me that something can be done to lighten the first steps of the beginner, and this is what I have tried to do. No practical art can really be taught; one man can only help another to learn; but it is common experience that such help will often save a great deal of trouble. Certainly no man ever learned to shoot by being lectured on the construction of a rifle, and yet such lectures are a regular part of musketry instruction. So far as I know, the experiment has never been made, in the case in hand, for the same purpose or in any very similar manner, though different parts of the subject have been touched upon by several writers, both English and American, on legal studies and literature, and notably by Kent. Possibly a connected account of the sources and authorities of English law, as they have come to be in modern practice, may be of interest to some of the Continental scholars, especially Frenchmen, who of late years have brought admirable industry and intelligence to bear on our methods of conducting both political and judicial affairs. But I have written, in the first place, for our own learners of the Common Law on both sides of the ocean, and my work stands to be judged by their proof in using it. If they find it useful I shall be well content, even more content than if I should perchance convince a mature philosopher or economist that the science of law has some right to exist.

It will be seen that the two parts of the book are to some extent independent of one another; and any reader who so chooses can, without much inconvenience, disregard the logical order of generality and take the second part first. However that may be, the combination of the two in one volume, and the preference of English examples and illustrations in the first part, are intended as a protest against the habit of regarding "jurisprudence" as something associated with a little knowledge of the laws of every country but one's own.

Some chapters and parts of chapters have already been printed in the *Harvard Law Review* for whose hospitality I hereby return my best thanks, and others in the *Law Quarterly Review*.

F. P.

CONTENTS

PART I

SOME GENERAL LEGAL NOTIONS

CHAPTER I

The Nature and Meaning of Law

CHAPTER II

Justice according to Law

CHAPTER III

The Subject-Matter of Law

CHAPTER IV

Divisions of Law

CHAPTER V

Persons

CHAPTER VI

Things, Events, and Acts

CHAPTER VII

Relation of Persons to Things: Possession and Ownership

CHAPTER VIII

Claims of Persons on Persons: Relation of Obligations to Property

PART II

LEGAL AUTHORITIES AND THEIR USE

CHAPTER I

The Express Forms of Law

CHAPTER II

THE SOURCES OF ENGLISH LAW

CHAPTER III

SOVEREIGNTY IN ENGLISH LAW

CHAPTER IV

CUSTOM IN ENGLISH LAW

CHAPTER V

LAW REPORTS

CHAPTER VI

Case-Law and Precedents

CHAPTER VII

Ancient and Modern Statutes

PART I

SOME GENERAL LEGAL NOTIONS

CHAPTER I

THE NATURE AND MEANING OF LAW

Difficulty of the most general ideas in all sciences.

WE find in all human sciences that those ideas which seem to be most simple are really the most difficult to grasp with certainty and express with accuracy. The clearest witness to this fact is borne by the oldest of the sciences, Geometry. No difficulty whatever is found in defining a parabola, or a circle, or a triangle. When we come to a straight line, still more when we speak of a line in general, we feel that it is not so easy. to be satisfied. And if it occurs to us to ask the geometer what is the relation of his "length without breadth" to the sensible phenomena of space, matter, and motion, we shall find ourselves on the verge of problems which are still too deep for all the resources of mathematics and metaphysics together. A philologist will be ready enough with his answer if we question him on the Greek or the Slavonic verb. If we ask him what is a verb in general we may have to wait a little, and if we ask him to account for language itself we shall find ourselves again in a region of doubt and contention. It is not surprising, then, that the student approaching the science of law should find the formal definiteness of its ideas to vary inversely with their generality. No tolerably prepared candidate in an English or American law school will hesitate to define an estate in fee simple: on the other hand, the greater have been a lawyer's opportunities of knowledge, and the more time he has given to the study of legal principles, the greater will be his hesitation in face of the apparently simple question, What is Law?

No complete theory of law without complete theory of society: but approximate generalisation needful.

In fact, a complete answer to this question is not possible unless and until we have a complete theory of the nature and functions of human society. Yet we cannot afford to wait for such a theory, for we are born into a social and political world from which we cannot escape. Rule, custom, and law beset us on every side. Even if at this or that point we go about to defy them we cannot ignore them; and the possible points of revolt, as reflection will show, are really but few even in such kinds of life as are called lawless. We have to abide the law whether we will or no; and to abide it, on the whole, in obedience rather than in resistance. The French Revolution seemed, and in many respects was, a fundamental catastrophe: but it appeared, as things resumed a settled frame, that a large proportion of French institutions, traditions of policy, and positive laws too, had survived the Revolution. If then we are to obey with understanding, we must endeavour to understand so much as is needful for the purpose in hand, relying on the most approximately certain data that we can command.

Society cannot exist without rules of social order.

Man cannot live alone; the individual cannot do without the family; and although family groups can be conceived as independent and self-sufficing, the family has from very early times been in like manner part of a larger society, whether it be a clan, a tribe, or a nation, with which it is bound up. No society can continue without some uniform practice and habits of life. Individual impulse has to be subordinated to this need; and this subordination is a never-ending process. Hence there must be rule and constraint; and not the less so because, in one sense, the aims of the society and of the individual coincide. On the whole and in the long run the interest of the individual is that society should exist. This is obviously true; but it is far from obviously true, indeed it seems not to be true, that his interest coincides always or everywhere with the interest of the society whereof he is a member, either as it really is or as it seems to be to those who conduct its affairs. Society comes into existence because its members could not live without it; but in continuing to exist it forthwith aims at an ideal, and that ideal is for the society and not for the individual member. The need for internal order is as constant as the need for external defence. No society can be stable in which either of these requirements substantially fails to be provided for; and internal order means a great deal more than the protection of individuals against wilful revolt or wanton lawlessness. Express and definite forms of association are required for the fulfilment of these purposes and the maintenance of a perpetual succession from one generation of men living in society to another. When established, these forms embody and preserve the individual character of every self-maintaining community. In the sum of such forms, as expressing and determining in each case the conditions of collective life and well-being, we have the State. We say well-being with reference to the ideal and not with reference to the actual success attained. Some States have secured the well-being of their members much better than others, and the less successful ones may be called relatively bad, or in some cases even very bad. Still an inferior social organisation, though measurably worse than other and better forms, is immeasurably better than none.

The State needs rules binding on citizens as such.

Further, if the State is to be permanent, we need more than the existence of some kind of social rule. We conceive many rules, the common and fundamental ones in matters of right and wrong, for example, to be binding on men simply as rational and social beings, without regard to any positive institutions. But this will not suffice for the State, which is an association for living together in definite ways. There must be rules binding the members of the State not merely as human or rational, but as members of that State; and this is not affected by the fact that to some extent, perhaps to a large extent, such rules include the matter of universal or more highly general duties which are of antecedent and independent force. Wherever any considerable degree of civilisation has been reached, we find means appointed by public authority for declaring, administering, and enforcing rules of this kind. In dealing with these rules, as with all others, both the persons administering them and those whose interests are affected have to attend not only to the rules or principles themselves, but to the conditions under which they become applicable, the mode in which they are applied, and the consequences of their application. The sum of such rules as existing in a given commonwealth, under whatever particular forms, is what in common speech we understand by law; the publicly appointed or recognised bodies which administer such rules are courts of justice. By justice, in this usage, we mean not only the doing of right, or the duty thereof, as between man and man, but the purpose and endeavour of the State to cause right to be done.

Such rules make up law.

Law not necessarily professional or official.

In modern times and in civilised countries we find the work of courts of justice carried on by permanent officers; it is a special kind of work, and the knowledge of law is a special kind of knowledge which can be acquired only by a professional training. Law has developed an art and a science of its own just as much as medicine. These conditions are now so usual that we might easily think them necessary; but they are not so.

Law and legal justice can exist without a profession of judges or advocates; and where a legal profession exists, its divisions, and the relation of its branches to one another, have varied and still vary to a wide extent in highly civilised countries and down to our own times. Thus at Rome under the later Republic and the early Empire there was a class of highly skilled advocates, and under the Empire there was something like a Ministry of Justice, but for a long time there was nothing answering to the ordinary judicial establishments of modern States. In England it does not appear that before the Norman Conquest there was any distinct legal profession at all, and in the succeeding Anglo-Norman period there were professional or at any rate skilled judges, but no professional advocates. In Iceland, about the same time, there was a highly technical system of law[1]; courts were regularly held, and their constitution was the subject of minute rules; and there were generally two or three persons to be found who had the reputation of being more skilled in law than their neighbours. Yet with all this there were neither judges nor counsellors in our modern sense. It is the ad-

[1] There is quite enough to support this statement apart from the elaborate pleadings set out in the present text of the Njáls Saga, which are believed to be of much later introduction.

ministration of justice with some sort of regularity that marks the existence of law, not the completeness of the rules administered, nor any official character of those who administer them.

Custom. There has been much discussion about the relation of custom to law. Custom, except in distinctly technical applications which are really part of a developed legal system, seems to have no primary meaning beyond that of a rule or habit of action which is in fact used or observed (we may perhaps add, consciously used or observed) by some body or class of persons, or even by one person. It was the "custom" of Hamlet's father to sleep in his orchard of the afternoon. In the *Morte d'Arthur* we constantly read of a "custom" peculiar to this or that knight; for example, Sir Dinadan had such a custom that he loved every good knight, and Sir Galahalt, "the hault prince," had a custom that he would eat no fish. And it is still correct, though less common than it was, to use the word in this manner. Often custom is the usage of some class or body less extensive than the State, such as the inhabitants of a city, the members of a trade. But it can have a scope much wider than the limits of the State. The Church, which of course is not bounded by any State, and in the medieval view could not be, had her own customs and refused to let any secular power pass judgment on their validity. No constant relation to law or judicial authority can be predicated of custom. It may or may not be treated as part of the law. Much law purports to be founded upon custom, and much custom has certainly become law. The extent to which this has happened, and the manner in which it has been brought about, are matters of history in the legal system which each particular State has developed or adopted. We shall have to return to this when we consider the sources and forms of the law of England. So far the word "custom" may be said to suggest the notion of potential or incipient legality. But on the other hand much custom is quite outside the usual sphere of law. Still the word has a certain ethical force tending to confine its use to those habits which the persons practising them recognise as in some way binding. Such are, to take a conspicuous example, customs of tribes and castes which have a religious character. "Customary" carries more weight, though it may be only a little more, than "usual [1]." In the weakest case we mean by custom a little more than

[1] See Littré, s.v. *Coutume*. Perhaps this tendency is more marked in French than in English.

habit, for one may have habits of an automatic or mechanical kind of which one is barely or not at all conscious. It is hardly needful to add that a great deal of law, at any rate of modern law, has not any visible relation to pre-existing custom.

"Practice," in the modern usage of the legal profession, signifies a particular kind of custom, namely, that by which a court of justice regulates the course of its own proceedings.

Moral law, natural law or law of nature.

We have used the word Law, so far, without any epithet, the sense in which we have used it being that which is commonly understood where nothing in the context requires a different one. But the word has other usages more or less analogous to the principal meaning. Moral law is the sum of the rules of conduct which we conceive to be binding on human beings, generally or with regard to the circumstances of a particular society, so far forth as they are capable of discerning between right and wrong; but it may also mean the rules to which the members of a particular society are actually expected, by the feelings and opinions prevalent in that society, to conform. Sometimes the distinction between actual and ideal rules of conduct is marked by speaking of moral rules, or of "positive morality," when we mean the rules accepted in fact at given times and places, but of "natural law" or "law of nature" when we mean such rules as are universally accepted, or in our opinion ought so to be. Positive morality may be, and in many times and places is known to have been or still to be, contrary to universal morality or natural law. The supposed duty of a Hindu widow to burn herself with her husband's corpse is a striking example.

The rules observed, or generally expected so to be, by the governments of civilised independent States in their dealings with one another and with one another's subjects are called the Law of Nations, or International Law. We are not called upon to consider here whether they are more nearly analogous to the law administered by courts of justice within a State, or to purely moral rules, or to those customs and observances in an imperfectly organised society which have not fully acquired the character of law, but are on the way to become law. This last mentioned opinion is my own; but I do not deem this a fit place for dwelling upon it. The whole matter is much disputed, and cannot be effectually discussed without assuming a good deal both of law and of the history of law to be known. Law of nations.

Bodies of rule or custom existing in a limited

Extended use of "law" for particular social rules.

section of a community, and enforced by the opinion of that section within itself, are often called laws: as when we speak of the laws of honour, or the laws of etiquette. It is to be remembered that in medieval Europe the "law of arms" was for the persons affected by it a true and perfect law, having its courts, judges, and compulsory sentences. In modern times this use of the word seems to be avowedly metaphorical. Sometimes we hear of "the code of honour," which cannot be justified even as a metaphorical license: a code, as we shall see later, being essentially a collection of articulate and definite rules or statements, and generally purporting to proceed from a definite authority.

"Law" in the concrete as an *enacted* rule.

In English we use the word Law in a concrete sense to mean any particular rule, having the nature of law in the abstract sense, which is expressly prescribed by the supreme power in the State, or by some person or body having authority for that purpose, though not generally supreme. A law, in this sense, is the exercise of a creative or at least formative authority and discretion; the power that made it might conceivably have chosen to make it otherwise. The rule is such because a definite authority has made it so; it lay in the lawgiver's hand what it should be. There is an element, at least, of origination. Application of existing principles, however carefully worked out, and however important it may be in its results, is not within the meaning. Therefore, although declarations of legal principles, or interpretations of express laws, by courts of justice may well be said to form part of the law, and so to be law in the abstract sense, we cannot say of any such declaration or interpretation that it is "a law."[1] When we are using the term in this concrete sense it is not only correct enough for ordinary political purposes, but correct without qualification, to say that "Laws are general rules made by the State for its subjects."[2] The plural "laws" is ambiguous, and the context must determine in which sense it is used. It may cover both meanings, as when we speak of "the laws of England" as including the whole body of English law, both what has been enacted by Parliament and what is derived from other sources. It is quite possible for the administration and development of "law" and the production of

[1] When some part of the general law has been designated by the context, it may afterwards be referred to as "a law," *i.e.* a portion of law, without reference to its being an express enactment or not, as if we say, "The law of slander by spoken words is not a reasonable law."

[2] Raleigh, *Elementary Politics*, ch. v. *init.*

concrete "laws" to be in the same hands to a greater or less extent. Thus a decision of an English Superior Court is law unless and until reversed or overruled by a higher Court; a rule of procedure made by the Judges under the powers conferred on them by the Judicature Acts is *a* law, though English-speaking lawyers do not commonly call it so, because it is more convenient to use the appropriate term "Rule of Court." In like manner an Act of the Imperial Parliament, or an Order in Council, or an Ordinance made by the Legislature of a Crown Colony, is a law, though almost always called by the more specific name.

"Laws" in extended sense of particular rules in non-judicial matters.

This concrete usage is extended to all sorts of express rules made and recorded for the guidance of human action in all sorts of matters, both serious and otherwise. Clubs and societies have their laws; there are laws of cricket and laws of whist. As might be expected, the distinction between the concrete and the abstract sense is not always exactly observed in popular usage. One might say without impropriety: "It is *a law* of journalism that an editor shall not disclose the authorship of an unsigned article without the writer's consent," although "rule" or "custom" would be more accurate.

English "law" includes "ius" and "lex."

It is proper to note that the ambiguity of the word *law* seems peculiar to English among the chief Western languages. Law in the abstract, the sum of rules of justice administered in a State and by its authority, is *ius* in Latin, *droit* in French, *diritto* in Italian, *Recht* in German. For the express rule laid down by an originating authority these languages have respectively the quite distinct words *lex, loi,*[1] *legge* (the French and Italian words being modern forms of the Latin one), *Gesetz*. Thus an Englishman tends, consciously or not, to regard enacted law as the typical form; it is hard for him not to identify laws (as the plural of "a law") with Law. Frenchmen and Germans, on the other hand, are more likely to regard *loi* or *Gesetz* as merely a particular form of *droit* or *Recht*, and not necessarily the most important form.

"Ius," etc. include "law" and "right."

On the other hand, these Latin and other names for law in the abstract (*ius, droit, diritto, Recht*) correspond also to our distinct English word

[1] In some French phrases *droit* and *loi* run into one another, *e.g.* "homme de loi." "Droit naturel" and "loi naturelle," "droit des gens," and "loi des nations," are convertible terms. The like laxity as between *lex, leges*, and *ius* is common in medieval Latin. In German, so far as I know, *Recht* and *Gesetz* are never interchangeable. *Gesetz* means a rule which is in fact, not only by right or wrong philosophic construction, "set" by a definite authority, and even in figurative uses this primary meaning is not lost sight of.

right in its substantive use. This leads to verbal ambiguities, and gives occasion for confusions of thought, which are perhaps not less inconvenient than any consequences of *law* having to stand for both *ius* and *lex* in our language.

Extended use of "law" in scientific terminology.

From the concrete use of the word *law* we have by extension the term "law" or "laws of nature" in the language of natural philosophy, or science as it is now commonly called, though in truth it is but one kind of science. Here the word has a wholly distinct meaning from those we have hitherto mentioned. It signifies any verified uniformity of phenomena which is capable of being expressed in a definite statement, and by "the laws of nature" we mean the sum of such uniformities known or knowable—in other words, the uniformity of nature as a whole. Doubtless this language originally implied a belief that uniformity in nature, whether general or particular, is due to will and design in some way analogous to those of human princes and rulers; but it has long ceased to have any such implication as a matter of necessity or even of common understanding.[1] No one thinks of Grimm's Law, or other "laws of phonetics," as anything but

[1] Cp. Mr. John W. Salmond on "The Law of Nature," *L. Q. R.*, xi. 121 142

compendious expressions of more or less generally observed facts in human speech, or in particular groups of languages. Further, this meaning has been carried back into the region of moral and political science, as when we speak of the laws of political economy or history. We may even say, if we please, though it would hardly be elegant, that the laws of history are exemplified in the history of law, thus using the word in the primary and the derivative sense in the same sentence. Here the term has quite lost its ethical associations; in fact those who insist most strongly upon the ethical element of law in its primary sense are perhaps those who are most likely to object to this usage. Such a phrase as laws of political economy, laws of history, laws of statistics, has no dependence whatever on any conception of a tribunal or a lawgiver, or of doing justice. It signifies only the normal results, as collected by observation or deduced by reasoning, of conditions, and (where human action is concerned) habits and motives, assumed to exist and to have effect. Whether we like those results or not; whether and to what extent the conditions are within the control of deliberate human action; and in what direction, if at all, we shall endeavour to modify the conditions or counteract the results,—may be matters deserving to be most carefully weighed: but they belong to a different order of considerations. Physicists have studied what are called the laws of electricity till it has become possible to light our houses with electric lamps. The occupier of a house so lighted can turn those laws to account whenever he pleases, and for so long as he pleases, provided that everything is in order, and in that sense he can control them. But his reasons for wanting or not wanting to light up a particular room at this or that hour have nothing to do with electrical science. The fact that a stone lies on the ground is an example of the "law of gravity." My desire to pick it up, followed by the act of picking it up, does not affect the "law,"—in other words, that particular aspect of the uniformity of nature,—in any way: it only varies the example. A well-to-do man going abroad lets his house to a friend at a nominal rent: the "laws of political economy" have nothing to say to this: the transaction is not such an one as economists contemplate. In short, the "laws of nature" are, for the lawyer and moralist, matters not of law at all in their sense, but of pure fact. And this applies equally to the so-called laws of human action in so far as human action is a subject of scientific observation.

Law in its compulsory aspect: Sanctions.

We may now leave aside the secondary and derivative meanings of "law" or "laws," and attend only to such rules as are recognised and administered in a commonwealth, and under its authority, as binding on its members. Thus far we have said nothing about the enforcement of the rules. In a modern civilised State it is well understood that, if resistance is made, the power of the State, or such part thereof as may be needful for the purpose, will be put forth to overcome it. Only the commonest knowledge of affairs and events, as they occur day by day, is required to assure us that the commission of acts forbidden by law, or disobedience to the orders of a court of justice, is likely to have unpleasant consequences in various degrees and kinds, according to the nature of the case and the system of law and government existing at the time and place, and that much work and thought are spent on behalf of the State in making that likelihood approach as near as may be to certainty. Common knowledge no less informs us, it is true, that the public servants of even the most highly organised State do not attain constant or uniform success in this endeavour. Some offenders escape and some laws are disregarded. But the State is, on the whole, prepared to compel its members to obey the law, and does, on the whole, exercise an effective compulsion; that is to say, it will and can make compliance with the law preferable to disobedience for most men on most occasions, by the application of fitting means through its officers appointed for that purpose. If this much cannot be affirmed in a given society at a given time (say a minor South American republic when a revolution is at its height), that society is in a condition of political anarchy for the time being, or at least the functions of the State are suspended. In fact we find the will and power to enforce the law by public authority to be stronger in proportion as the commonwealth is more settled, more prosperous, and more refined. "The magistrate beareth not the sword in vain." Hence it is natural for men living in a civilised State to regard this public will and power of causing the law to be observed as belonging to the very essence of law. The appointed consequences of disobedience, the *sanctions* of law as they are commonly called, seem to be not only a normal element of civilised law, but a necessary constituent. Law without a sanction, and that sanction in the hands of the State, can, in this way of thinking, easily appear like a contradiction in terms.

Enforcement of law by the State is relatively modern.

Any such view, however, will be found hard to reconcile with the witness of history. For we find, if we look away from such elaborated systems as those of the later Roman empire and of modern Western governments, that not only law, but law with a good deal of formality, has existed before the State had any adequate means of compelling its observance, and indeed before there was any regular process of enforcement at all. We have already vouched the Icelandic Sagas to show that law can do without a legal profession: we may vouch them to show no less clearly that it can do without a formal sanction. More than this, we find preserved among the antiquities of legal systems, and notably in archaic forms and solemnities, considerable traces of a time when the jurisdiction of courts arose only from the voluntary submission of the parties: and this not only as between subject and subject, but as between a subject and the State[1]. We need not doubt that effectual motives for submission could be brought, sooner or later, to bear on unwilling subjects. The man who did not submit himself to law could not claim the benefit of the law; there was no reason

[1] The history of English criminal procedure affords at least one striking illustration; but I purposely avoid a digression.

why every man's hand should not be against him. Outlawry, now all but obsolete even in name, was the formal expression of the archaic social rules by which law was gradually made supreme. Again, archaic procedure shows us a period in which a suitor may obtain judgment, but must execute the judgment for himself. The most the State will do for him is to come eventually to his aid if the adversary or the adversary's friends continue to deny him right. In the meantime private force holds the ground, but the winning suitor's private force is lawful and the loser's is unlawful.

At this stage the State can hardly be said to provide any sanction of its own; it only gives moral support and coherence to sanctions already existing in a vague form. Conversely, one of the first signs of the reviving power and solidity of the State in the early Middle Ages was the jealous restriction of private force, even when the claimant who sought his ends by might had full right on his side. *Iniuste* and *sine iudicio* became convertible terms. It is wrong to do oneself right without judgment and public authority.

Informal sanctions common to law and morality.

In one sense we may well enough say that there is no law without a sanction. For a rule of law must at least be a rule conceived as binding; and a rule is not binding when any one to whom it applies is free to observe it or not as he thinks fit. To conceive of any part of human conduct as subject to law is to conceive that the actor's freedom has bounds which he oversteps at his peril. One or more courses of action may be right or allowable; at least one must be wrong. Now what is felt to be wrong is felt to call for redress. This may be direct or indirect, swift or tardy; but in the mere sense and apprehension of redress to come, however remote and improbable it may seem, and however uncertain the manner of it may be, we have already some kind of sanction, and not the less a sanction because its effect may be precarious. All this applies to moral no less than to legal rules. Taken thus largely, there are sanctions of infinite degrees from obscure monitions of conscience to general and open reprobation, or even acts of violence prompted by the indignation of one's fellow-men [1]; and, if we pass from the moral and social to the legal sphere, from some small expense or disadvantage in the conduct of a lawsuit, or some small penalty for delay in performing a public duty, to the severest penalties of criminal

[1] Such acts may or may not be justifiable, and the rule enforced may or may not be itself right from the point of view of universal morality. This does not concern us here.

jurisdiction. But in a modern State the sanction of law means both for lawful men and for evil-doers something much more definite. It means nothing less than the constant willingness and readiness of the State, in the persons of its magistrates and officers, to use its power in causing justice to be done; and this in respect not only of the main duties enforceable by law, but of an immense number of incidental and at first sight arbitrary rules and conditions.

Law and the "will of the State."

In short the conception of law, many of its ideas, and much even of its form, are prior in history to the official intervention of the State, save in the last resort, to maintain law. True it is that in modern States law tends more and more to become identified with the will of the State as expressed by the authorities intrusted with the direction of the common power. But to regard law as merely that which the State wills or commands is eminently the mistake of a layman, as one of the greatest modern jurists has hinted[1]; and, we may add, of a layman who has not considered the difference between modern and archaic societies, or the political and social foundations of law. For most practical purposes the citizens

[1] Ihering, *Geist des römischen Rechtes*, i. 37 (ed. 1878).

of a State, and to a considerable extent, though not altogether, lawyers and magistrates also, have not to concern themselves with thinking what those foundations are. Their business is to learn and know, so far as needful for their affairs, what rules the State does undertake to enforce and administer, whatever the real or professed reasons for those rules may be. Moreover, criminal law, which is eminently imperative, is that branch of law which appeals most to the popular imagination, and fills the largest place in popular notions of legal justice. Again, the unexampled activity of the legislative power in modern States has largely increased the sphere of express enactment. All these causes have made it possible and even plausible to regard law not only as being embodied in the commands of a political sovereign, but as consisting of such commands and being nothing else. They have not altered the fundamental facts of human society; and the merely imperative theory of legal institutions remains as one-sided and unphilosophical as it was before. Law is enforced by the State because it is law; it is not law merely because the State enforces it. But the further pursuit of this subject seems to belong to the philosophy of Politics rather than of Law.

CHAPTER II

JUSTICE ACCORDING TO LAW

Conditions for existence of law: possible anomalous cases.

THE only essential conditions for the existence of law and legal institutions are the existence of a political community and the recognition by its members of settled rules binding upon them in that capacity. Those conditions are present in all societies of men who are not mere savages. Even among civilised men, on the other hand, they may be suspended in particular circumstances. We can get one example by supposing a boat's crew from a wrecked ship, made up of different nationalities in about equal proportions, to land on an island in the high seas which is neither occupied nor claimed by any civilised Power. Such a party would, it is conceived, be remitted to what was once called "the state of nature," aided by whatever conventions they might agree upon as appropriate to their situation. A lawyer would probably advise them to consider themselves as still under the law of the ship's flag, but it is difficult to say that this or any other law would have any real authority apart from the agreement of the whole party. Practically the law of nature, or in less ambiguous terms the common rules of civilised morals and the dictates of obvious expediency, would have to suffice for the present need. Again, it is not very difficult for civilised men to find themselves, without any violent accident, in places where it is hard to say whether any and, if any, what law prevails in the ordinary sense. Take the case of an English or American traveller, or an Englishman and an American travelling together, in the region of the Khaibar Pass beyond the British frontier post at Fort Jamrud and before Afghan territory is reached. Certainly they are not subject to the law of British India; still less, if possible, to the law of Islam as applied in Afghanistan. Yet the persons and property of those who go up the Pass on the appointed days and with the proper escort are really safer than they would be in some parts of almost any European or American city But peculiar phenomena of this kind, which are transitory accidents as compared with the ordinary course of civilised life, do not affect the normal formation and effects of civilised law, nor throw any light on its origin. If, on the other hand, a new social combination which at first sight may have been precarious becomes permanent, its members acquire, either by convention or by submission to an existing jurisdiction, some permanent form of government and law. The inchoate stages of this process (which, in fact, has taken place in various parts of the world, such as the extreme Western States of America, within living memory) are interesting in their own way, but are hardly within the province of the lawyer. Settled rules and recognised jurisdiction are the lawyer's tests.

Justice

Law presupposes ideas, however rudimentary, of justice. But, law being once established, *just*, in matters of the law, denotes whatever is done in express fulfilment of the rules of law, or is approved and allowed by law. Not everything which is not forbidden is just. Many things are left alone by the State, as it were under protest, and only because it is thought that interference would do more harm than good. In such things the notion of justice has no place: the mind of the State is rather expressed by Dante's "guarda e passa."

The words "just" and "justice," and corresponding words in other tongues, have never quite lost ethical significance even in the most technical legal context. The reason of this (unduly neglected by some moderns for the sake of a merely verbal and illusive exactness) is that in the development of the law both by legislative and by judicial processes appeal is constantly made to ethical reason and the moral judgment of the community. Doubtless the servants of the law must obey the law, whether specific rules of law be morally just in their eyes or not: this, however, is only saying that the moral judgment we regard is the judgment of the community, and not the particular opinion of this or that citizen. Further, some conflict between legal and moral justice can hardly be avoided, for morality and law cannot move at exactly the same rate. Still, in a well-ordered State such conflict is exceptional and seldom acute. Legal justice aims at realising moral justice within its range, and its strength largely consists in the general feeling that this is so. Were the legal formulation of right permanently estranged from the moral judgment of good citizens, the State would be divided against itself.

We may better realise the fundamental character

Order, not compulsion, the fundamental character of law.

of law by trying to conceive its negation or opposite. This will be found, it is submitted, in the absence of order rather than in the absence of compulsion. An exercise of merely capricious power, however great in relation to that which it acts upon, does not satisfy the general conception of law, whether it does or does not fit the words of any artificial definition. A despotic chief who paid no attention to anything but his own whim of the moment could hardly be said to administer justice even if he professed to decide the disputes of his subjects. The best ideal picture I know in literature of what might be called natural injustice, the mere wantonness of power, is exhibited in the ways of Setebos as conceived by Robert Browning's *Caliban.*[1] In the same master's *Pippa Passes*, the song of the ancient king who judged sitting in the sun gives a more pleasing though not a more perfect image of natural or rather patriarchal justice. Absence of defined rule, it must be remembered, is not the same thing as the negation of order. The patriarch may not do justice according to any consciously realised rule, and yet his decrees are felt to be just, and will go to the making of rules of justice for posterity.

[1] "As it likes me each time I do: so He."

Relation of singular acts of sovereign power to law.

It is true that even in highly civilised States we meet with occasional or singular acts of sovereign power which are outside the regular course of justice and administration, and which nevertheless must be counted as laws. In form they do not differ from the ordinary acts of the law-making authority; and in substance they are laws in so far as they affect in some way the standing of individual citizens before the law, must be regarded and acted upon by the judges and other public servants of the State, and will at need be put in force by the executive. In some of these cases there is really nothing abnormal except the form of the transaction. What began with being a special exercise of supreme power for a special occasion has settled into a routine which, though in form legislative, is in substance administrative or judicial, or partly the one and partly the other. Such is the case in this country with the private Acts of Parliament by which railway and other companies are incorporated and have powers of compulsory purchase and the like conferred on them. So, before the establishment of the Divorce Court, the dissolution of marriages by a private Act of Parliament was a costly and cumbrous proceeding, but still of a judicial kind. In these and similar cases the form of legislation has been rendered necessary by historical or constitutional accident. Sometimes, again, the purpose of these extraordinary legislative acts is to relieve innocent persons, and those who may have to derive titles to property from them, from the consequences of some venial failure to comply with the requirements of law. Marriages between British subjects have often been celebrated in good faith, but in fact without authority, by British Consuls and other official persons in remote parts of the world, and on the error being discovered Acts of Parliament have been passed to give validity to marriages so celebrated. Acts of indemnity have much the same nature, so far as they relate to the neglect or omission of requirements which have come to be regarded as merely formal. When the Test Acts were in force there was an annual Act of Indemnity for the relief of those public officers (being in fact the great majority) who had not performed and observed all the conditions which at one time had been supposed, and for a time possibly were, needful precautions for securing the Protestant succession to the throne. Lastly, that which in form is an act of legislation may be a more or less thinly disguised act of revolution, civil war, or reprisal against unsuccessful revolution. Acts of attainder are the best English example in this kind.[1] All these matters have their own historical and political interest: but we have nothing to learn from them about the normal contents and operation of legal institutions. The Roman name of *privilegia* marks them off as standing outside the province of regular and ordinary law.

Normal marks of law: Generality.

Let us pass on, then, to consider what are the normal and necessary marks, in a civilised commonwealth, of justice administered according to law. They seem capable of being reduced to Generality, Equality, and Certainty. First, as to generality, the rule of justice is a rule for citizens as such. It cannot be a rule merely for the individual: as the medieval glossators put it, there cannot be one law for Peter and another for John. Not that every rule must or can apply to all citizens; there are divers rules for divers conditions and classes of men. An unmarried man is not under the duties of a husband, nor a trader under those of a soldier. But every rule must at least have regard to a class of members of the State, and be binding upon or in respect of that class as determined by some definite position in the community.

[1] They must be carefully distinguished from impeachment, which is a regular process known to the law, though an unusual one.

This will hold however small the class may be, and even if it consists for the time being of only one individual, as is the case with offices held by only one person at a time. Certain rules of law will be found, in almost every country, to apply only to the prince or titular ruler of the State, or to qualify the application of the general law to him. In England, again, the Prince of Wales, as Duke of Cornwall, is the subject of rules forming a singular exception to the general law of property; and the Lord Chancellor has many duties and powers peculiar to his office. But these rules are not lacking in the quality of generality, for in every case they apply not to the individual person as such, but to the holder of the office for the time being. They may be anomalous with regard to the legal system in which they occur; and, like other rules of law, they may or may not be expedient on the particular merits of each case. They are not in any necessary conflict with the principles of legal justice merely because they are of limited or unique application.

Equality. Next, the rule of generality cannot be fulfilled unless it is aided by the principle of equality. Rules of law being once declared, the rule must have the like application to all persons and facts coming within it. Respect of persons is incompatible with justice. Law which is the same for Peter and for John must be administered to John and to Peter evenly. The judge is not free to show favour to Peter and disfavour to John. As the maxim has it, equality is equity.[1] So much is obvious and needs no further exposition. But it may be proper to point out that the rule of equality does not exclude judicial discretion. Oftentimes laws are purposely framed so as to give a considerable range of choice to judicial or executive officers as to the times, places, and manner of their application. It is quite commonly left to the judge to assign, up to a prescribed limit, the punishment of proved offences: indeed, the cases in which the court is deprived of discretion are exceptional in all modern systems. Apart from capital offences, there are only one or two cases in English criminal law where a minimum punishment is imposed, and none, it is believed, where there is no discretion at all. Certain remedies and forms of relief, in matters of civil jurisdiction, are said to be discretionary as contrasted with those which parties can demand as their right. Still, a judicial discretion, however wide, is to be

[1] The working use of the maxim is not quite so simple as this.

exercised without favour and according to the best judgment which the person intrusted with the discretion can form on the merits of each case.[1] Differences of personal character and local circumstances are often quite proper elements in the formation of such a judgment, but any introduction of mere personal favour is an abuse. We still aim at assigning equal results to equal conditions. Judicial discretion is not an exception to the principle of equality, but comes in aid of it where an inflexible rule, omitting to take account of conditions that cannot be defined beforehand, would really work inequality. This implies that only such conditions are counted as are material for the purposes of the rule to be applied. Of course no two persons or events can be fully alike. What rules of law have to do is to select those conditions which are to have consequences of certain kinds: which being done, it is the business of the courts to attend to all those conditions, and, saving

[1] In various cases where the risk of discretion being perverted by outside influence or pressure has seemed greater than that of spontaneous partiality, the holders of discretionary power or authority are deliberately exempted from being called on to give an account of their reasons. In such cases the discretion is said to be not judicial, but absolute. Examples: the protector of a settlement, the governing bodies of schools under the Public Schools Act.

judicial discretion where it exists, not to any others. A plaintiff who argues his case in person may be tedious and offensive, but the judge must nevertheless do him justice as fully as if his argument were excellent. This may seem too obvious for statement in England, but there are parts of the British Empire where it is not, or within recent times was not, so. Suppose, on the other hand, it were a rule of law that no man who wore a white hat before May-day could take a legacy within the year. It would not be competent to any court to say that, as between A and B, rival claimants for the same legacy, the legacy should be paid to A, notwithstanding that he had worn a white hat in April, because he was a poor man and more in want of money than B. The law cannot make all men equal, but they are equal before the law in the sense that their rights are equally the subject of protection and their duties of enforcement.

Certainty: scientific character of law.

Further, as the requirement of generality leads to that of equality, so does the requirement of equality lead to that of certainty, which brings in its train the whole scientific development of law. We must administer a general rule, and administer it equally. There can be no law without generality;

there can be no just operation of law without equality. But we cannot be sure of a rule being equally administered at different times and in the cases of different persons unless the rule is defined and recorded. Justice ought to be the same for all citizens, so far as the material conditions are the same. Now to carry out this idea the dispenser of justice ought to be adequately furnished with two kinds of information. He should know what is accustomed to be done in like cases, and whenever new conditions occur he should know, or have the means of forming a judgment, which of them are material with a view to legal justice, and which are not. Moreover, there must be some means of securing an approximate uniformity of judgment; otherwise judges and magistrates of all degrees will make every one a law of his own for himself, and the principle of equality will not be satisfied. Justice dealt out according to the first impression of each particular case, the "natural justice" of an eastern king sitting in the gate, is tolerable only when the community is small enough for this function to be in the hands of one man, or very few, and its affairs are simple enough for offhand judgments not to produce results of manifest inequality. This is as much as to say that in a civilised commonwealth law must inevitably become a science. The demand for certainty becomes more exacting as men's affairs become more complex, and the aid of the courts is more frequently sought. Trade and traffic, in their increasing volume, speed, and variety of movement, raise new questions at every turn, and men expect not only to get their differences settled for the moment, but to have solutions which will prevent the same difficulties from giving trouble again. How far would natural justice carry us, for example, towards a settlement of the problems involved in making contracts by letter, telegraph, or telephone? Hence law becomes an artificial system which is always gathering new material. The controverted points of one generation become the settled rules of the next, and fresh work is built up on them in turn. Thus the law is in a constant process of approximation to an ideal certainty which, by the nature of the case, can never be perfectly attained at any given moment. Every one who has studied the law knows that the approximation is apt to be a rough one, and is exposed to many disturbing causes. We shall see something, in the latter part of this work, of the methods by which it is effected in the system of the Common Law. Meanwhile it is to be remembered that the political sciences do not claim to be exact in either a speculative or a practical point of view. For the practical purposes of a State governed according to law, that degree of certainty suffices which will satisfy the citizens that the law works on the whole justly and without favour; and in archaic societies not only is a pretty rough kind of certainty sufficient, but no other is possible.

Certainty of law limited by attainable certainty of facts.

Rules of law have to be applied to the facts ascertained by the tribunal. Now the facts are often in dispute; indeed those cases are a small minority where there is a real difference between the parties, and that difference turns merely upon the application of the law to undisputed facts.[1] And the process of forming a judgment as to the truth of the facts, where conflicting accounts are offered, is itself an approximate one at best for human faculties. In early stages of legal institutions we find that there is hardly so much as a serious attempt in this direction; the matters at issue are disposed of by methods which seem to us at this day not only artificial and inadequate,

[1] Much of the work done by the machinery of justice consists in enforcing just claims to which there is no defence; but mere refusal or neglect to pay one's debts without compulsion of law does not constitute a real matter in difference.

but out of all relation to any grounds of reasonable conclusion. The task would indeed seem to have been thought above the power of mortals. Ordeal in its various forms is a direct appeal to supernatural aid in the supposed incompetence of human understanding. Proof by oath, where the oath is conclusive, a procedure of which the medieval "compurgation" is the best known example, is the same thing in a milder form. Wherever and so long as the facts cannot be ascertained with any precision, there is no occasion for precise or elaborate rules of law. The law cannot be more finely graduated than the means of ascertaining facts; and the judicial investigation of facts with something approaching completeness and exactness dates only from relatively modern times. Hence the development of law is largely bound up with the development of procedure. As improved procedure enables the law to grapple with complex facts, the aspirations of lawyers and citizens are enlarged, and they are by no means content to aim at the minimum of certainty which will ensure public acquiescence in the justice of the State, and a tolerable average of obedience. On the contrary, they will aim (as men do in every science and art, when once they become seriously interested in it) at an ideal maximum. But even in the most advanced polity we shall find now and then that the subtilty of forensic and judicial thought outruns the possibilities of effectual inquiry and administration. Questions are sometimes put to juries which it is hardly possible for any one not learned in the law to see the point of.

Law a distinct science: not co-extensive with ethics.

In assuming a scientific character, law becomes, and must needs become, a distinct science. The division of science or philosophy which comes nearest to it in respect of the subject-matter dealt with is Ethics. But, though much ground is common to both, the subject-matter of Law and of Ethics is not the same. The field of legal rules of conduct does not coincide with that of moral rules, and is not included in it; and the purposes for which they exist are distinct. Law does not aim at perfecting the individual character of men, but at regulating the relations of citizens to the commonwealth and to one another. And, inasmuch as human beings can communicate with one another only by words and acts, the office of law does not extend to that which lies in the thought and conscience of the individual.

The possible coincidence of law with morality is limited, at all events, by the range of that which theologians have named external morality. The commandment, "Thou shalt not steal," may be, and in all civilised countries is, legal as well as moral: the commandment, "Thou shalt not covet," may be of even greater importance as a moral precept, but it cannot be a legal one. Not that a legislator might not profess to make a law against covetousness, but it would be inoperative unless an external test of covetousness were assigned by a more or less arbitrary definition; and then the real subject-matter of the law would be not the passion of covetousness, but the behaviour defined as evincing it.[1] The judgment of law has to proceed upon what can be made manifest, and it commonly has to estimate human conduct by its conformity or otherwise to what has been called an external standard. Action, and intent shown in acts and words, not the secret springs of conduct in desires and motives, are the normal materials in which courts of justice are versed, and in the terms of which their conclusions are worked out and delivered. With rare exceptions,[2] an act not other-

[1] The saying ascribed (it seems apocryphally) to Dr. Keate of Eton: "Boys, if you're not pure in heart, I'll flog you," exemplifies in a neat form the confusion of external and internal morality.

[2] Those exceptions are perhaps of an accidental and not very substantial kind; but, after all corrections and allowances, "malice" does sometimes in English law mean evil motive, such

wise unlawful in itself will not become an offence or legal wrong because it is done from a sinister motive, nor will it be any excuse for an act contrary to the general law, or in violation of any one's rights, to show that the motive from which it proceeded was good. If the attempt is made to deal with rules of the purely moral kind by judicial machinery, one of two things will happen. Either the tribunal will be guided by mere isolated impressions of each case, and therefore will not administer justice at all; or (which is more likely) precedent and usage will beget settled rule, and the tribunal will find itself administering a formal system of law, which in time will be as technical, and appeal as openly to an external standard, as any other system. This process took place on a great scale in the formation of the Canon Law, and on a considerable scale in the early history of English equity jurisdiction.

Law cannot enforce all moral rules, but may sometimes react on the moral standard.

Besides and beyond the limitation of the field of law to external conduct, there are many actions and kinds of conduct condemned by morality which for various reasons law can either not deal with at all or can deal with only in an inci-

as personal enmity or vindictiveness. For further consideration of intention and motive see ch. vi., p. 138 below.

dental and indirect manner. It would be the vulgarest of errors (as we have already hinted) to suppose that any kind of approval is implied in many things being left to the moral judgment of the community and to such pressure as it can exercise. Law does not stand aside because lawgivers or judges think lightly of such things, but because, whether from permanent or from transitory causes, the methods of legal justice are not appropriate for dealing with them, and the attempt to apply those methods would, so far as it could be operative at all, probably do more harm than good. At the same time rules of law may well have, in particular circumstances, an effective influence in maintaining, reinforcing, and even elevating the standard of current morality. The moral ideal present to lawgivers and judges, if it does not always come up to the highest that has been conceived, will at least be, generally speaking, above the common average of practice; it will represent the standard of the best sort of citizens. This is especially the case in matters of good faith, whether we look to commercial honesty or to relations of personal confidence. With few exceptions, the law has, in such matters, been constantly ahead not only of the practice but of the ordinary professions of business men. We have similar results on a more striking scale when a law which is not indigenous brings in with it the moral standards on which it is founded. Thus a good deal of European morality has been made current in India by the Anglo-Indian codes; and European morality itself has been largely moulded not only by the teaching of the Christian Church, but by the formal embodiment of that teaching in both ecclesiastical and secular laws. The treatment of homicide by early English criminal law was founded on the extremely strict view taken by the Church of the guilt of bloodshedding; and the extinction of duelling in this country seems to be due, in no small part, to the steady refusal of English law to regard killing in a duel, even without any circumstances of treachery or unfairness, as anything else than murder. We are not speaking here of the mere fact that persons abstain from unlawful conduct through dread of the legal consequences, a fact which, taken by itself, has no moral significance at all.

Legal rules in things morally indifferent.

Again, rules of law differ from rules of morality in excess as well as in defect. It is needful for the peace and order of society to have definite rules for a great many common occasions of life, although no guidance can be found in ethical reasoning for adopting one rule more than another. There is no law of nature that prescribes driving on either the right or the left-hand side of the road, as is plainly shown by the fact that our English custom to take the left-hand side is the reverse of that which is observed in most other countries. But in a land of frequented roads there must be some fixed rule in order that people who meet on the road may know what to expect of one another. And, the rule being once fixed either way for the sake of general convenience, we are bound in moral as well as in legal duty to observe the rule as we find it. On much the same footing are the rules which require particular forms to be observed in particular transactions, for the purpose of making the proof of them authentic and easily found, or in the interest of the public revenue, or for other reasons. There are not many such cases in which the form actually imposed by the law can be said to be in itself the only appropriate one, or obviously much better than others that might be thought of. But, since it has been thought fit to require some form, it is necessary that some one form should be authorised. Here, too, the choice between courses which in themselves were morally indifferent is determined by the law, and thenceforth it is the moral as well as the legal duty of every one concerned, if he will act as a good citizen and a prudent man, to do things in the appointed manner and form.

Legal responsibility without moral fault in certain cases.

But there is more than this. As in many cases acts and conduct that are morally blameworthy must go quit of anything the law can do, so in many cases, on the other hand, persons are exposed, for reasons of public expediency, to legal responsibilities which may or may not be associated with moral fault, and which cannot be avoided even by the fullest proof that in the particular case the person who is answerable before the law was morally blameless. A man may, of course, make himself answerable by his own promise for many things independent of his moral deserts or even wholly beyond his control: but we are here speaking of liability not assumed by the party's own act and consent, but imposed by a rule of law which does not depend on any one's assent for its operation. Thus a man is liable in most civilised countries for the wrongful acts and defaults of his servants in the course of their employment, whatever pains he may have taken in choosing competent servants and giving them proper instructions. Obviously this is a hard rule for the employer in many cases; but its existence in every system of law shows that in the main it is felt to be just. Again, both Roman and English law have made owners of buildings[1] responsible, in various degrees, for their safe condition as regards passers-by in the highway, or persons entering them in the course of lawful business; and this without regard to the amount of the owner's personal diligence in the matter. Again, questions often arise between two innocent persons, of whom one or other must bear the loss occasioned by the wrongful act of some one from whom redress cannot be obtained; as when a man who has obtained goods by fraud from their owner sells them to an unsuspecting third person, and then absconds, leaving nothing behind him. Here the original owner and the buyer may be equally free from fault, but they cannot both have the goods, and the price cannot be recovered. Hardship to one or the other is inevitable.

In all these cases the loss or damage, as between the two innocent parties who are left face to face, may be considered as accidental. The rule of law has to determine as best it can on which side the loss shall fall; and, since by the hypothesis neither party has incurred moral blame, and this is the

[1] This is by no means the full measure of the rule in our law. For simplicity's sake only part of it is now stated.

very cause of the difficulty, it is plain that the rules of ordinary social morality will afford no guidance. We have to resort either to considerations of general public expediency, or, if no obvious balance of convenience appears either way, to the purely technical application of rules already settled in less obscure matters. And this last method is not a mere evasion of the problem, but is a reasonable solution so far as no stronger reason can be assigned to the contrary. For the principle of certainty requires that a rule once settled shall be carried out to its consequences when no distinct cause is shown for making an exception or revising the rule itself. If any sense of hardship to the individual citizen remains after these considerations have been weighed, and it has also been observed that citizens have an equal chance of benefit as well as burden under special rules of this kind, it may be said that exposure to this kind of liability is part, and not a large part, of the price which the individual has to pay the State for the general protection afforded by its power, and the general benefit of its institutions.

Development of law necessarily artificial.

Thus neither the work nor the field of legal science can be said to coincide with those of any other science. And the development of this, as of all other distinct branches of science, can be carried on only by the continuous effort of persons who make it the chief object of their attention in successive generations. This has been recognised in the institutions, both practical and academical, of all civilised nations. A civilised system of law cannot be maintained without a learned profession of the law. The formation and continuance of such a learned class can be and has been provided for, at different times and in different lands, in various ways which it does not now concern us to mention in detail. It is not necessary for this purpose that the actual administration of justice should be wholly, or with insignificant exceptions, in the hands of persons learned in the law, though such is the prevailing tendency of modern judicial systems. It is enough that the learned profession exists, and that knowledge of the law has to be sought, directly or indirectly, in the deliberate and matured opinion of its most capable members. And the activity of modern legislation makes little or no difference to this: for we are not now speaking of the general policy of the lawgiver, which in a free country is and must be determined not by any one class, but by the people through their representatives. The office of the lawyer is first to inform the legislature how the law stands, and then, if change is desired (as to which he is entitled to his opinion and voice like any other citizen), to advise how the change may best be effected. Every modern legislature is constantly and largely dependent on expert aid of this kind. A well-framed Act of Parliament, whatever amount of novelty it may contain, is as much an application of legal science as the considered judgment of a court. Legislation undertaken without legal knowledge is notoriously ineffectual, or, if not ineffectual, apt to create new troubles greater than any which it cures. There is no way by which modern law can escape from the scientific and artificial character imposed on it by the demand of modern societies for full, equal, and exact justice

CHAPTER III

THE SUBJECT-MATTER OF LAW

Contents of law: duties of subjects.

RULES of law being the rules which are deemed binding on members of the State as such, and are administered, as and because thus binding, by courts of justice, we have next to see of what kind are the contents of those rules. It seems that we may describe them, in the most general terms, as the duties of subjects under the common authority of the State, together with the conditions by which those duties are defined and made capable of application. We speak here of subjects, not citizens. For there are members of the State who by reason of natural or conventional disability (which may be temporary or permanent) do not enjoy full political rights: and there are strangers who dwell for a longer or shorter time in the jurisdiction of the State without being or becoming members of it. Persons in either of these positions, as they are admitted to the benefit and protection of the laws, are likewise expected to conform to them: that is to say, they are not the less subjects because they are not or cannot be citizens. It would not be correct, however, to say that alien residents within a State are altogether subject to the same duties as citizens; for they may be and often are exempt from some duties on particular grounds of policy, and from others because they are not capable of the office or station to which those duties are annexed. Hereafter we shall find it convenient to use the term "citizen" as including all subjects unless the stricter meaning is indicated.

Duty, positive and negative.

We ascribe duty to any one who is bound by a rule. Every such person's duty is to conform to the rule. If the rule is one which courts of justice administer, the duty is a legal one. Such duties alone being within our present scope, it will be understood that others are not included in the term unless it is expressly qualified: similarly of rights. Duty may be active or positive—that is, the rule may require a person bound by it to do something in the way either of some definite action or of a continued course of action. A parent is bound to maintain his children, a debtor to pay his debt at the proper time, or when demanded. Or it may be a passive or negative duty—that is, the rule may forbid something from which a person bound by it must abstain. Thus we must all abstain from theft and other criminal offences; and in the sphere of voluntary choice negative undertakings are common, as when an actor engaged for a particular theatre binds himself not to act elsewhere, or a retiring partner not to compete with the firm. A positive duty may carry negative duties with it as a necessary accompaniment. If Peter has bound himself by a lawful contract to sell his house to John, he must hand over possession to John at the proper time, and in the meantime he must not sell or convey the house to any one else. Performance is the more appropriate word for the fulfilment of positive duties, observance for negative ones; but this nicety of language is not always regarded.

Only negative duties are strictly enforceable.

Strictly speaking, law cannot compel the performance of positive duties. A negative duty can be directly enforced by physical constraint, or by otherwise depriving a man of the means of action. But a positive duty can be enforced only in an indirect manner, by attaching such consequences to non-performance as to make performance in most cases and for most persons the preferable course. In this sense a man may and often does act under compulsion of law, but he cannot really be compelled to act. Where the performance consists in the payment of money which the party bound has sufficient means to pay, or in the delivery of specific property which is in his possession, it may be within the power of the law to do what he ought to have done—that is, to take from the debtor's property the amount due and pay it to the creditor, or to put a purchaser in possession of the property to which he is entitled, or otherwise as the case may be. How far this can be done in any particular system of law depends not only on what is physically possible, but on the authorised methods of procedure and execution. Similarly there may be power (and there is now in England) to appoint some one to do any formal act which ought to be done by the party, and which he refuses to do. But a performance requiring personal skill, such as the singing of a part in an opera, or the painting of a picture, obviously cannot be compelled by any normal human power. Again the observance of a negative duty cannot become impossible except by an actual breach, which may or may not render subsequent observance impossible according to the nature of the facts: but the possibility of an active duty being performed is subject to many accidents, which moreover may be beyond the parties' control. If a man has promised to pay a thousand pounds six months hence, and has lost all his property, with or without his own fault, before the day comes, it is plain that his creditor cannot be paid. *Ex nihilo nihil fit.* Again the performance of any duty that involves personal skill or attention may be frustrated by illness or other misadventure disabling the party. These matters, however, belong to the machinery of law and the adjustment of remedies rather than to the elementary substance of duties and rights.

Right: indeterminate as freedom, or determinate as claim or power.

Right is the correlative of duty. As duty is a burden imposed by law, so right is freedom allowed or power conferred by law. Every right implies duty somewhere: but it must be noted that we speak of right sometimes in a determinate and sometimes in an indeterminate sense. For it is commonly said that a man has a right to be free from assault and unwarranted imprisonment, to deal with things belonging to him (within certain limits) as he will, and so forth: and whatever tends to abridge legal freedom or interfere with its exercise is said to diminish a man's rights, or to be an invasion of them. These rights have not answering to them any particular determinate duty of this or that citizen; nevertheless they are more than bare liberty or power. The fact that I can do as I please until some superior force or irremovable obstacle hinders me is a merely natural fact, and law has nothing to say to it. So far as actual power or freedom from restraint in doing this or that act is concerned (say, taking fish in a particular month, or travelling to London to give evidence before a Royal Commission), it is all one whether there is no law bearing on the matter, or a law which disallows the act if done in some other way or at some other time, but allows it now and thus, or a law which encourages it, as by authorising payment of a witness's travelling expenses. The act may be right in the popular and rudimentary sense of not being forbidden, but freedom has not the character of legal right until we consider the risk of unauthorised interference. It is the duty of all of us not to interfere with our neighbour's lawful freedom. This brings the so-called primitive rights into the sphere of legal rule and protection. Sometimes it is thought that lawful power or liberty is different from the right not to be interfered with; but for the reason just given this opinion, though plausible, does not seem correct. There is more than this when any subject wrongfully meddles with another's person or property; he forthwith incurs the specific duty of making just compensation, and the other acquires the specific right of calling for the same. This right is not merely freedom, but a definite claim, the power of getting one's due by process of law: it is what our law calls a right of action. On the other side the duty is no longer general, but has regard to a determinate claim of some one interested in its performance; it loses in extension but gains in intension. There is not only a right but a claim, not only duty but liability.

Generally the power of enforcing a rule of law belongs to those for whose sake it exists, and as against whom it has been broken. But the power and the benefit need not be co-extensive. In many branches of law the State, through its public officers, assumes the power of setting the law in motion, sometimes exclusively, sometimes concurrently with the person aggrieved: sometimes any citizen whatever is authorised to take proceedings of his own motion. It would not be correct, however, to say that right is more extensive than duty in such cases: rather the same facts may produce several duties or liabilities. There seems to be no valid reason against ascribing rights to the State in all cases where its officers are enjoined or authorised to take steps for causing the law to be observed, and breakers of the law to be punished.

No duty without right, though some duties without determinate correlative rights.

If this last statement is accepted, there will be no occasion to say, as is often said, that there are duties without any correlative rights. Doubtless there are duties without any determinate rights corresponding to them: indeed, this is the case, in any view, with the negative duties which we owe to the community at large. For my duty not to damage other people's goods, for example, is one duty, not millions of separate duties owed to every one who has anything to be damaged, or in respect of every separate chattel of any value. Positive duties of a public kind, such as the duty of paying taxes, or serving on a jury, or aiding to keep the peace when called on by an officer of justice, are in the same plight. So are duties towards, or rather in respect of irrational animals, inasmuch as they cannot exercise rights;[1] and so were duties in respect of slaves in systems of law which recog-

[1] If there were any purpose to be served by it, there would be no more difficulty in enabling proceedings to be taken, by a legal fiction, in the name of an animal as plaintiff or prosecutor than there was in taking formal criminal proceedings against animals, of which there are many medieval examples.

nised slavery. Under any of these conditions it seems more reasonable and more in accordance with the current usage of speech to say that the right correlative to the duty is in the hands of the State than to say that there is none. Where the State acts in the manner of a creditor and for the direct benefit of the public revenue, as in collecting taxes, still more, where it acquires and deals with specific property in the way of buying, holding, and selling, it seems that the State has rights in the fullest sense. But this cannot be adequately considered without reference to the doctrine of legal personality.

Can the State have duties?

Whether the State can have duties has been a point fruitful of discussion, though the point is perhaps of no great practical importance. It is clear that the person or body holding supreme political power in a commonwealth (assuming that there is such a person or body) has only to use that power to be legally free. No less clear is it by experience that while claims against the State are made in various ways more difficult to maintain than claims against private members of the State, yet in the practice of civilised nations claims which are in substance against the State are dealt with by courts of justice, and lead, if the claim is made good, to redress being granted out of public funds. But this is compatible with the view that the State submits these questions to its own tribunals only as a matter of grace and favour, though the grace may be so customary that citizens look on it as a political and moral right. And that is certainly the view which the forms and rules of our own law have embodied. Moreover, we said that the primary mark of rules of law is to be binding on citizens as such. The State is not a citizen nor an aggregation of citizens, and a system of law can quite well exist without the State ever being considered to be legally bound towards a citizen. All jurisdiction, nevertheless, appears to have begun in consent, and all government ultimately rests on consent; not in the sense that it was ever founded by express convention, but that no government can in the long run be carried on against the dissent of an effective majority. Therefore it seems hard to say that the State cannot by its own consent be really subject to rules of law so long as that consent is in force. In practice individual citizens may count on the submission of the State to its own tribunals (whatever the extent of it may be) not being arbitrarily revoked. The security is the same, in the last resort, that we have for the due administration and enforcement of the ordinary law binding on subjects. Moreover, persons and bodies representing the State in various departments of its functions may well come before the law in a position not necessarily distinguishable from that of ordinary citizens. But this again brings us to the question of legal personality which still lies ahead.

According to that view of the nature of law which regards it as the command of a supreme political authority and nothing else, it is difficult to ascribe rights, and barely possible to ascribe duties, to the State. But as we do not consider such a view to rest on any sound foundation, we are not concerned here with its consequences. If we accept Hobbes's derivation of the State and all civil order from an original covenant by which every man surrendered his natural right or power into the hands of a sovereign person or body from whom all law thenceforth proceeds, we must accept likewise the consequences which Hobbes deduced and set forth once for all:[1] otherwise not.

Can a man have rights against himself?

It seems at first sight a paradox to say that a man can have rights against himself. The moral duties which are called self-regarding are so far

[1] *Leviathan*, ch. xxvi., cp. ch. xxix.

recognised by criminal law that some of the grosser breaches are punishable; but one cannot claim redress from oneself, in other words a right of action against oneself is not possible. Again a man may in the exercise of his lawful freedom confer many rights on others which limit that exercise in various ways and for periods of varying duration; but the duties are binding on him just because the rights are not in his own control but belong to the other parties. Yet it is conceivable and possible that a man should initiate compulsory proceedings against himself: as when, as the law of some countries now allows, a drunkard enters of his free will a licensed institution for the treatment of dipsomania, and, having so entered it, may lawfully be detained for a certain time notwithstanding any attempted revocation of his consent. In such a case the patient is after a sort his own accuser and judge; and as this power of self-restraint is conferred for his own benefit, we cannot but allow that he exercises a right. Both the right and the corresponding duty of submitting to the self-imposed restraint are called into existence by the party's own option. From the moral point of view we should say that a man in this condition is really divided against himself, and that the law, taking notice of this abnormal fact, enables him to strengthen his better against his worser self. In ethics all duties have regard to oneself in some sense. As there is no necessary question of an external tribunal, even the most informal, or of external acts or consequences, there is no real difficulty about this. If we speak of "duty towards God," we introduce an approach to the legal conception of duty; the Supreme Being (or, in polytheistic religions, a superior being determined as appropriate to the occasion by particular functions or attributes) taking the place of an external human lawgiver, or of the State. And in fact it may be observed that moral rules which belong exclusively or eminently to definite religious systems have ever tended to assume a formal and legal character. Ethical feeling (where it survives this treatment) has to be satisfied and reinforced by counsels of perfection and other forms of aspiration to an ideal beyond and outside the rules.

Wrong. Wrong is in morals the contrary of right. Right action is that which moral rules prescribe or commend, wrong action is that which they forbid. For legal purposes anything is wrong which is forbidden by law; there is wrong done whenever a legal duty is broken. A wrong may be described, in the largest sense, as anything done or omitted contrary to legal duty, considered in so far as it gives rise to liability. Hence the existence of duty, as it involves right, involves also the possibility of wrong; logically no more than the possibility, though we know too well that all rules are in fact sometimes broken. Duty, right, and wrong are not separate or divisible heads of legal rules or of their subject-matter, but different legal aspects of the same rules and events. There may be duties and rights without any wrong; this happens whenever legal duties are justly and truly fulfilled. There cannot, of course, be a wrong without a duty already existing, but wrongs also create new duties and liabilities. Strictly speaking, therefore, there can be no such thing as a distinct law of wrongs. By the law of wrongs we can mean only the law of duties, or some class of duties, considered as exposed to infraction, and the special rules for awarding redress or punishment which come into play when infraction has taken place. There is not one law of rights or duties and another law of wrongs. Nevertheless there are some kinds of duties which are more conspicuous in the breach than in the observance. The natural end of a positive duty is performance. A thing has to be done, and when it is duly done the duty is, as we say, discharged; the man who was lawfully bound is lawfully free. We contemplate performance, not breach. Appointments to offices are made, or ought to be, in the expectation that the persons appointed will adequately fulfil their official duties. When I take a ticket from London to Oxford, I hope and expect that the railway company will convey me safely and punctually to Oxford. The same may be said of negative duties which are annexed to positive ones, or have been assumed by the party's own undertaking. But when we come to negative duties imposed by the general law, we find our attention directed to the event of their violation. For the elementary duties we owe to all men have no natural end short of life's end itself. An honest man is always observing the duty of not stealing, and has never done observing it so long as he lives honestly. There is nothing to fix the mind's eye to one moment of negative observance more than another. Dramatic incidents of resistance to temptation make no difference in the legal view. A man can do no more than observe the rule, and ought to do no less, whatever the additional moral merit of resisting temptation may be. Therefore it is the breach of such duties that gives us a defined point of concentration, and in practice we approach the conception of the duty through the fact of the wrong done. Again the term *wrong* suggests not only a right violated, but some one's right, in the full and determinate sense of that word, to redress; although what is really correlated to the injured person's right to redress is not the wrong itself, but the new duty and liability arising from it. Thus we have in English usage a tendency, first to limit the word *wrong*, in legal speech, to cases where a general duty is broken, and, further, to use it by preference in cases where the enforcement of the law rests with the injured person in the first instance, or altogether, and not with the officers of the State. Great authors in our law, Hale and Blackstone, have spoken of "Public Wrongs," but it is more usual to speak of crimes or offences.

Arrangement by duties or rights.

We may shortly sum up the result of the preceding discussion by saying that there is no harm in taking the conception of Duty for our clue or basis of classification in dealing with some groups of legal rules, that of Right in dealing with others, and for others again that of Wrong, determined by reference either to the duty disregarded or to the right violated. The matter is essentially one of convenience. Only we must remember that in this we are not dividing the actual contents of legal rules, but distinguishing aspects, and making sometimes one and sometimes another prominent as it suits us. Duty and Right are not really more divisible in law than action and reaction in mechanics. Hence it would seem that such topics of discussion as whether a system of law should be arranged under heads of duties or heads of rights are at best of secondary importance, and cannot lead to conclusions of any universal validity. The practical lawyer's instinct is to regard anxious dwelling on these topics with a certain impatience, an impatience that may be said to border on contempt. If he is pressed for reasons, and ventures to give them offhand, his reasons are perhaps more likely to be bad than good. Yet reflection appears to show that in this as in many other cases the practical instinct is in the main justified, although it may be long before the justification is made explicit in a form that will satisfy philosophers. Experience builds better than it knows.

Auxiliary rules of law.

So far as it is worth while to indicate any general preference in classification, and other things being equal, duties appear to come in the natural and logical order before rights, for it is of the essence of law to assign rules of conduct, and a rule of conduct which did not affirm some kind of duty would not be a rule. This is more clearly seen in the case of moral rules. No one would think of treating morality as a system of rights. However that may be, there is more than duties and rights to be taken into account before we have covered the subject-matter of jurisprudence: and this to such an extent that we should still be left very far from a complete system of law if we were furnished with an exhaustive list of all the legal rules which can be said in any natural sense to declare duties or affirm rights. Duties and rights are mere disjointed parts of an organism, so to speak, until we know how they are connected with the acts and events of human life. They are attached to certain persons; they have their modes of beginning and of continuance assigned by rules of law, and there are other rules according to which they cease. A mere detached knowledge of the contents of legal rules would be of little use without knowing the conditions which determine their application. In order to have any real working acquaintance with a system of law we must inquire, not only what duties and rights are recognised, but how rights are acquired and lost; what rights are capable of transfer, and how; by what acts and events duties are imposed; how far and in what ways duties can be transmitted; and how they are discharged. The conditions defining these things are therefore, as mentioned at the beginning of this chapter, an integral part of the subject-matter of law, and the rules which declare them are among the most important. Some branches of the law may be said, indeed, almost to consist of rules of this kind. They set forth the conditions on which rights and duties depend, but they do not for the most part declare any right or duty in the first instance. When a man attains full age is a very practical question, and the statement that in England every one under the age of twenty-one years is an infant is certainly a proposition of law; but it does not state any duty or right. Legal capacity is not a right, still less is the want of it a wrong. Persons dealing with infants are subject to risks and duties which may be learnt from other sources; the rule only tells us who is an infant. Again, we are all bound to respect the rights of ownership; owners are also subject to a variety of special duties. To bring the legal rules of conduct into relation with actual facts we have to know how people become owners, and how ownership and other interests in property are transferred. It is often much easier to know what are the owner's rights, whoever he may be, than to know who the owner is. Again, every man is bound to pay his debts, and this, viewed from the other side, is the creditor's right to be paid. But what is to happen if the debtor dies, or the creditor? What becomes of the duty and the claim? In the literature of English law the exposition of this and other incidental matters fills two large but by no means diffuse volumes, well known to lawyers as "Williams on Executors." Without a body of rules to determine title and succession the law of property would be in the air. Especially does this hold in that most important and difficult part of the law of property which deals with Possession. In almost every branch of the law Possession may have far-reaching and decisive consequences. The legal idea of Possession, though based on elementary facts of human nature and society (or rather, perhaps, because so based), is among the highest and hardest we have to grapple with. But the practical consequences in a given system of law depend largely on the rules that determine how possession is acquired, transferred, and lost. Ultimately rules of this kind enable us to fix the duties and rights of parties in the particular cases. They exist for the sake of ascertaining rights and duties. But they do not, in the first instance, affirm any specific right or duty. We may conveniently call them "determining" rules when we desire to speak of them by a compendious name.

Rules of evidence and procedure.

Further, rules of law are rules in and for a living commonwealth, active and operative precepts, not merely contemplative propositions. In Professor Holland's happy phrase, law has to deal with rights in motion as well as at rest. Duties have to be enforced and rights have to be vindicated. Beyond this, modern courts of justice devote much of their best labour and skill to quiet non-contentious or not fully contentious work of which the public at large, with its dramatic and criminalist view of legal proceedings, is almost unaware. The administrative business of courts of equity and probate jurisdiction is of this kind. Such work is directed to defining and preserving the rights of parties rather than enforcing them. In many cases there is no hostile contention at all; the parties only want to be certified what their rights are. In these processes, as well as in the coarser and more conspicuous ones of litigation between adversaries, duties and rights are constantly modified and transformed. One duty or set of duties is discharged or extinguished and another arises. After judgment given the duties and claims are not the same as before. There is a new duty, that of satisfying the judgment. And herein the State, through its judicial and executive officers, has its own active and more or less independent part, at least in all modern systems.

Thus we need a whole machinery of auxiliary rules[1] to guide the citizen in seeking the aid of courts of justice, and to regulate the powers and discretion of the court itself. In criminal affairs the need is no less. The commonwealth is supreme and can punish offenders, but it must punish according to law. Nay, we require security that penal law shall be abundantly just. It is better that some offenders should go scot-free than that condemnation and punishment should seem

[1] Procedure has been judicially described as "the mode of proceeding by which a legal right is enforced, as distinguished from the law which gives or defines the right, and which by means of the proceeding the Court is to administer,—the machinery as distinguished from its product:" Lush L.J. in *Poyser* v. *Minors* (1881), 7 Q.B. Div. 329, 333.

arbitrary. When we consider a system of law from the citizen's point of view rather than the lawyer's, as a material element in the political stability of the commonwealth, we may almost say that certainty in procedure is more important than certainty in the substance of law.

Substantive and Adjective Law.

We see then that the mere sum of existing duties and rights is not the law, nor even a separable or working portion of the law. It is but one element, the positive or static element as one might call it. In order to build up the organic life of law we have need of the genetic element, the principles which determine the positive rules in their concrete application to persons, acts, and events; and of the dynamic element, the rules whereby legal consequences are made manifest and worked out. Positive rules of law tell us what is just; determining rules (which we might also call the law of Title, using that word in the largest sense) point out what is the justice of the case in hand; the rules of procedure show us how justice is to be done.

What we have spoken of as the positive law of duties and rights is commonly called Substantive Law. The law of "determining" rules, which has not in English any technical or generally accepted name, is usually and conveniently treated as auxiliary to the substantive law, and attached, for purposes of exposition and reference, to its various heads. Thus the Law of Vendors and Purchasers (that is, of land and interests in land, as the term is always understood among English-speaking lawyers)[1] is dealt with as a branch of the law of Real Property.

For equally good reasons of convenience Procedure is dealt with as a topic apart. Codes of civil and criminal procedure are in force in the majority of civilised countries, including British India. Here in England we have the substance of a code of civil procedure, though not the name, in the Rules of the Supreme Court. Procedure, considered in its relation to substantive law, has been conveniently called Adjective Law by modern writers.

[1] It would be natural enough for a continental jurist left to himself in an English law library to turn to a treatise on Vendors and Purchasers in the expectation of finding something about the sale of goods, or to a treatise on the Contract of Sale for information about the transfer of land in English-speaking countries. In either case he would be signally disappointed. The reasons of this are historical and, from the philosophic point of view, accidental.

CHAPTER IV

DIVISIONS OF LAW

Divisions of legal classification are formal, not material.

It is not possible to make any clear-cut division of the subject-matter of legal rules. The same facts are often the subject of two or more distinct rules, and give rise at the same time to distinct and different sets of duties and rights. The divisions of law, as we are in the habit of elliptically naming them, are in truth divisions not of facts but of rules; or, if we like to say so, of the legal aspects of facts. Legal rules are the lawyer's measures for reducing the world of human action to manageable items, and singling out what has to be dealt with for the time being, in the same way as number and numerical standards enable us to reduce the continuous and ever changing world of matter and motion to portions which can be considered apart. Thus rules of law can no more give us a classification of human acts or affairs than the rules of arithmetic can give us a classification of numerable things. In scholastic terms, the divisions of law are not material but formal. Practising lawyers do not concern themselves much with divisions of a high order of generality. They have to think, in the first place, of speedy and convenient reference, and the working arrangements of professional literature are made accordingly. So the types in a printing office are arranged not in order to illustrate the relations of spoken sounds or the history of the alphabet, but so that the compositor may lay his hand most readily on the letters which are oftenest wanted. Ambitious writers have sometimes gone to work as if it were possible to reduce the whole contents of a legal system to a sort of classified catalogue where there would be no repetitions or cross references, and the classification would explain itself. Ambition on that scale is destined to disappointment by the nature of things.

Classical or received divisions: impersonal and personal duties or rights.

Some general divisions in the science of law have been made classical by the method adopted in the Institutes of Justinian, and by the subsequent development given to the Roman ideas by commentators and modern jurists. One such division, which has been made explicitly prominent only in recent times, is now commonly marked by the terms *in rem* and *in personam*. Some duties and rights consist in a claim of one certain person upon another; the duty and the correlated right are alike determinate. In these cases the duties and rights are said by modern writers to be *in personam*. Other duties and rights do not import any such definite correlation. When we put ourselves in the position of duty, we find no certain person having the right; when we put ourselves in the position of right, we find no certain person owing the duty. These impersonal rights and duties, regarding all one's fellow-subjects or a class of them, are said to be *in rem*. We have already seen something of this in endeavouring to fix the conception of legal right. The reason why we cannot well use the English adjectives "real" and "personal" for this purpose is that they are already appropriated to special technical uses with which this would clash. It would be free from objection, however, to speak of personal and impersonal duties or rights.

Transition from *in rem* to *in personam*: Contract Obligation, Ownership.

The most obvious and typical example of an event creating rights *in personam* is a contract. John and Peter agree that John shall sell his house to Peter on certain terms. This gives John and Peter certain rights against each other; they are bound to one another by a tie of mutual claims existing between them and between them only. This definite relation of claim and duty was called an *obligation* by the Roman lawyers, and is still so called everywhere, save that in English-speaking countries an unfortunate habit has arisen of using "obligation" in a lax manner as co-extensive with duties of every kind.[1] Now let Peter pay John the purchase money, and John do all proper acts for completing the sale. Suppose, to simplify the illustration, that John has received the money in coin, and Peter has entered into the house and occupies it. Peter is owner of the house, and John and all other persons are under the duty of respecting his rights as owner, that is, of abstaining from trespass and the like. The money is John's, and Peter and all other persons must respect John's ownership of the money by not stealing it or otherwise meddling with it in any unauthorised way. These rights have no determinate corresponding duties, only the general duty of all men not to trespass, steal, and so forth. That duty in turn is not

[1] In English law the word formerly had a much more restricted meaning, namely the special kind of contract also called a bond. But the English name "bond" is now always or almost always used for this, and it is convenient to restore "obligation" to its Roman sense, for which there is no synonym.

correlated to Peter's or John's rights more than to those of any other owner. *Dominium* is the Roman term for the rights of an owner against all the world: and the contrast of *dominium* and *obligatio* is the nearest approach that can be made, in classical Roman language, to the distinction marked by the modern terms *in rem* and *in personam*.

Obligation by wrong-doing.

Let us now take a further step. Robert, a stranger, wantonly or out of spite breaks a window in Peter's house. He has disregarded the general duty of respecting other men's property, and he incurs a new duty, that of making compensation to Peter. It may be that he is also liable to fine or imprisonment for the disturbance of public order involved in his wrongful act, but that is a distinct and different matter. On the other side, Peter has a personal and determined right against Robert. A legal bond of liability and claim has been created; that is to say, there is an obligation. If Peter comes out of the house at the moment when Robert breaks the window, loses his temper, and knocks down Robert, he has in turn broken in Robert's person the general duty of not assaulting one's fellow-subjects: for the right of action he has acquired against Robert is a right to redress by lawful means only, of which means knocking down the wrong-doer on the spot is not one in this case. Robert may not be held entitled to much compensation, but he is entitled to some. Here is yet another obligation, the liability being on Peter and the claim with Robert; and it results from a breach of the most general kind of duty, a duty corresponding to a so-called "primitive" right.

Personal duties other than obligations.

Obligation does not however include the whole of duties and rights *in personam.* There are personal relations recognised by law and having important legal consequences, but outside the legal conception of obligation. Peter, let us assume, lives in the house with his wife Joan, and they have children. Peter and Joan owe duties to one another which they cannot owe to any one else; and the same may be said (omitting minor distinctions in this place) of the duties existing between Peter and his children. But these duties are not reckoned as obligations: for they cannot be expressed as definite claims, and their performance cannot be reduced to any definite measure. They are fully discharged only when the relation out of which they arise has come to an end: in the case of marriage by death, or, in systems of law where divorce is allowed, by divorce. In the case of parental relations the normal mode of determination is the attainment of full age by the child (which, however, often has not that effect in archaic systems, and had not in the classical Roman law), to which many systems add marriage in the case of daughters, and adoption into another family.

Relations of this kind, moreover, are intimately associated with moral duties which are not capable of legal definition and perhaps not of precise definition at all. Lying thus on the borderland of morality and law, they give rise in law to duties and rights which resemble obligations in being personal, but differ from obligations, and resemble duties and rights *in rem*, in not being capable of exhaustion by definite assignable acts, or by any number of such acts. The resulting duties are determinate as to persons, but not determinate as to contents.

Duties which are impersonal or *in rem* answer, as we have seen, partly to particular and acquired rights of other persons, such as owners, partly to the so-called primitive rights which are universal. They may be duties to all one's fellow-subjects or only to some of them.

Creation of duties and rights by will of parties.

Impersonal duties and rights are always attached by rules of law to some condition or state of facts. Whether the conditions are to any extent under the control of the parties or not, the legal consequences are what the law makes them. By the mere fact of being a citizen or subject one is entitled to a certain measure of personal security, freedom to follow one's lawful calling, and so forth. By the fact of becoming an owner one acquires the rights and faculties of an owner, such as the law declares them to be. One may choose to avail oneself of them or not, but one cannot alter them. If one could, one would be able to impose new duties on one's fellow-citizens without their consent, in fact to make new law for one's own benefit. But this would contradict the fundamental purpose of law and justice. It is exactly what they aim at preventing.

Personal duties dependent on will of parties.

Personal duties and rights, on the other hand, may not only arise from acts of the parties, but be directly created and determined by their will. The parties to an agreement not only confer and assume duties by their voluntary act, but by the same act prescribe what the duties shall be.

The same remark applies to transactions involving agreement and obligation, though not usually included under the name of contract, such as the creation of trusts in English law. The parties can make a law for themselves just because their dispositions are personal to themselves, and do not impose or affect to impose any new duties on their fellow-subjects at large.

Personal duties prescribed by law.

Personal duties are also prescribed by rules of law and attached to acts or relations of parties. Sometimes they are contemplated by the parties, though not within their control, and sometimes not. Thus in the case of marriage and other family relations the legal consequences are contemplated and accepted, but cannot be framed and varied at the will of the parties like the duties created by a commercial contract.[1] In many cases where duties resembling those created by contract are imposed by law (where in Roman terms there is obligation *quasi ex contractu*), they are such as it is considered that a just man, on being fully informed of the facts, would in the circumstances willingly assume. The most familiar example in this kind is the duty of returning a payment made by mistake. Where obligation arises from a merely wrongful act, the liability is of course not desired by the wrong-doer, and is contemplated, if at all, as an evil (from his point of view) to be endured only so far as it cannot be avoided.

[1] This does not apply to incidental dispositions of property such as are made by marriage settlements. These may well be treated, as in our law they are, as matters of agreement largely within the control of the parties.

Liability by breach of agreement.

We have not yet mentioned another way in which personal duties and liabilities arise, namely from the breach of antecedent personal duties created by agreement.

Every such breach of duty is in some sense wrongful; and it is contrary to the original intention of the parties. Agreements are made in order to be performed, not to be broken. It is even possible to regard the breach of a promise as a wrong in the strictest sense, a trespass or deceit.[1] Still there is a good deal of difference. Duties under agreement may easily be broken without any wrongful intention. Performance may be prevented by misadventure (which is not always an excuse even if the party be not in fault), or there may be honest and serious diversity of opinion as to what is really due. Then, although parties do not desire their agreements to be broken, it would be incorrect to say that they never contemplated it; for they often make special provision for such an event, and even fix beforehand the amount or scale of the compensation to be paid. Thus it appears that the duty of compensation in case of non-performance is fairly regarded as incident and supplementary to the primary duty of performance. In practice and

[1] This is fully exemplified in the history of the Common Law.

practical exposition it would not be convenient, indeed it would hardly be possible, to separate the legal results of breach of contract from the rules determining what are the duties and rights of the parties before any breach.

Importance of distinction between self-prescribed and other duties.

From the point of view of a modern lawyer conversant with modern habits of life and business, it may well seem that the distinction between duties and rights prescribed by the parties themselves and those prescribed by the law is really of greater importance than that which looks only to their impersonal or personal character. The relations recognised by law can be divided, with no great apparent inequality as to quantity or value in human affairs, into those which arise from contract (or voluntary dispositions analogous to contract) and those which are independent of contract. And the distinction is at first sight so clear as to seem unmistakable. But the history of the law shows us that an absolutely clear-cut division is not to be had, even so, between the facts and relations to which our rules apply.

Roman meaning of "action."

The description of legal duties and rights as being *in rem* or *in personam* is usually and correctly said to be unauthorised by classical Latin usage. Roman lawyers spoke of "actiones," not "iura," being *in rem* or *in personam*. But it should be remembered that in Roman usage "action" included what we now call a "right of action," any determinate claim to some form of legal redress. "Action" was defined as a man's right of obtaining by process of law what is due to him, not as the process itself. "Nihil aliud est actio quam ius quod sibi debetur iudicio persequendi."[1] Hence the modern usage is not so wide apart from the Roman as it appears at first sight to be.

Public and Private Law.

A classical division accepted by almost all systematic writers is that of Public and Private Law. No rule of law can be said, in the last resort, to exist merely for the benefit of the State or merely for the benefit of the individual. But some departments of legal rules have regard in the first instance to the protection and interests of the commonwealth, others to those of its individual members.

In the former case the public interest is immediate; it can be directly represented by the proper officers of the State, and vindicated by them in the name of the State, or of its titular head: in the latter the interest of the individuals whose rights are affected comes in the first line;

[1] Celsus, D. 44, 7, de obl. et act. 51.

it is protected by the law, but the parties interested are left to set the law in motion. Rules of private law may be said to have remained in a stage where all rules of law probably were in remote times: that is to say, the State provides judgment and justice, but only on the request and action of the individual citizen: those who desire judgment must come and ask for it. Accordingly the special field of such rules is that part of human affairs in which individual interests predominate, and are likely to be asserted on the whole with sufficient vigour, and moreover no public harm is an obvious or necessary consequence of parties not caring to assert their rights in particular cases. In the law of contract and its various commercial developments these conditions are most fully satisfied; though even here considerations of "public policy," to use the accustomed English term, are by no means absent. In the law of family relations and of property motives of legitimate private interest have a considerable part, but they are not so uniformly operative that they can be treated as adequately guarding the interest of the commonwealth. Hence we find that theft and certain other forms of misappropriation and fraud, and even certain kinds of breach of contract, are punishable as public offences. The general security of property has to be considered as well as the chances of restitution in each case, which often are so slender that the person robbed or defrauded has no sufficient motive of self-interest for vindicating the law. When we come to bodily safety, the public interest balances, or in some cases even outweighs, the private. Wrongs of violence are in all civilised legal systems dealt with as offences against the commonwealth, in addition to the rights to redress which may be conferred on the individual injured. Incorporeal personal wrongs, such as defamation, afford a kind of neutral ground where the rights of the State and of individuals have about equally free play in modern law. There fall more specially under rules of public law the duties and powers of different authorities in the State, making up what is usually known as the law of the Constitution; also the special bodies of law governing the armed forces of the State, and the administration of its other departments; laws regulating particular trades and undertakings in the interest of public health or safety; and in short all State enterprise and all active interference of the State with the enterprises of private men. We say active interference. For there are many dispositions in particular departments of private law which are founded on reasons of public policy, but are left for the parties who may profit or be relieved by them to bring to the notice of the Courts. Of this kind are certain special restrictions on freedom of contract. In countries under the common law the State does not interfere of its own motion to prevent an agreement from being enforced on the ground that it is "in restraint of trade." On the other hand there are many legislative enactments which expressly or by necessary implication forbid certain kinds of contracts to be made. Such enactments appear to belong to public law, though it is often convenient or necessary to consider them in connection with the rules of private law whose usual operation is excluded or limited by them.

To public law, too, belong all the minor penal enactments incident to constitutional and departmental legislation. But public law does not even here hold the field alone, for the same legislation which creates new public duties and imposes penalties may well, under specified conditions, also confer new rights to redress on individuals either expressly or as a consequence of principles recognised by the courts.

The extent and effect of any such principles

cannot be laid down beforehand: it depends on the forms, methods, and history of the particular system of law which is being administered. In our law the violation of a public duty may often give a right of action to a citizen who has thereby suffered damage, but this is by no means an universal or necessary result.[1]

It will be seen therefore that the topics of public and private law are by no means mutually exclusive. On the contrary their application overlaps with regard to a large proportion of the whole mass of acts and events capable of having legal consequences.

The State as a party.

Sometimes the distinction between public and private law is made to turn on the State being or not being a party to the act or proceeding which is being considered. Only dealings between subject and subject, it is said, form the province of private law. But this does not seem quite exact: unless indeed we adopt the view, which has already been rejected, that the State is wholly above law and legal justice, and neither duties nor rights can properly be ascribed to it. Many valuable things both immovable and movable are held and employed for the public service: palaces, museums,

[1] *Ward* v. *Hobbs* (1878), 4 App. Ca. 13.

public offices, fortifications, ships of war, and so forth; in some countries railways and all the various furniture and appurtenances of these. Whether they are held in the name of the State itself, or of the head of the State, or of individual officers of the State or persons acting by their direction, is a matter of detail which must depend on the laws and usages of every State, and may be determined by highly technical reasons. In substance the State is and must be, in every civilised community, a great owner of almost every kind of object. Now the rights attaching to the State in this respect, or to the nominal owners who hold on the State's behalf, need not differ from those of any private owner, and in English-speaking countries they do not. They can be and are dealt with by the ordinary courts in the same way as the rights of any citizen, and according to the ordinary rules of the law of property for the preservation and management of the kind of property which may be in question. Again many persons have to be employed, and agreements to be made with them; and these transactions are judged, so far as necessary, by the ordinary rules of the law of contract. Now the rules mentioned not only belong to private law but are at its centre; they are the most obvious examples of what private law includes. It would be strange to say that they become rules of public law because the property and undertakings in question are public. The true view seems to be that the State, as an owner and otherwise, can make use of the rules of private law, and become as it were a citizen for the nonce, though ultimately for public purposes.

Use of "public" and "private" by writers on International Law.

Sometimes the law of nations is brought under the head of public law; this is plausible according to the test of the State being a party, which, however, we have not accepted. It is enough to say here that the duties of independent States to one another, whatever may be the extent of their analogy to legal duties, are not legal duties or the subject of legal rules in the sense now under consideration. On the other hand there is in modern law a body of principles and rules by which the courts are guided in deciding, on occasion, how far they are bound to take notice and make application of rules belonging to foreign systems of law; as where different stages of a transaction have taken place in different jurisdictions. These rules apply largely to matters of private law, and the principles are not confined to any particular local system. Differences of opinion exist among the learned, and the opinions of different writers or schools may prevail with the tribunals of different countries: but it is recognised on all hands that uniformity is desirable, and is to be aimed at as far as possible. Hence the sum of such rules is now commonly called Private International Law. This term has been much discussed, and by some competent persons vehemently disapproved,[1] but it would not be to the present purpose to enter upon the controversy, which assumes an advanced knowledge of law. What is here sought is merely to make a common modern term intelligible.

Roman division of law regarding Persons, Things, Actions.

Another classical division adopted by the Institutes of Justinian from Gaius is that which treats the whole body of law (that is, legal rules) as relating either to Persons, Things, or Actions.[2] "Omne autem ius quo utimur vel ad personas pertinet vel ad res vel ad actiones."

To a certain extent this division coincides with the division already noted of Substantive and Adjective law. The law of Actions is the body of rules determining the modes and processes of legal redress; it is equivalent to what modern writers call the law of Procedure, but with some addition of the law of Remedies: for, as pointed out above,

[1] See Holland, *Jurisprudence*, ch. xviii.

[2] Cp. Maine, *Early Law and Custom*, ch. xi., and Dr. Moyle's introduction to the first book of the *Institutes*.

the Romans hardly distinguished the right to a certain kind of redress from the process of obtaining it. So far there is nothing calling for fresh explanation; it is to be remembered, however, that, as Maine has pointed out, the distinction of substantive from adjective law must in ancient times have involved a much higher effort of abstraction than we can easily realise now. When we consider the further division of substantive law into law of Persons and law of Things, we are struck by the fact that the division, though not in terms confined to private law, has in fact been so confined by the usage of both ancient and modern expounders. It will appear shortly that there is good reason for this.

Practical point of the division.

Like the other divisions we have been considering, this is a division of legal rules, not of the facts to which they apply. It seems to be closely related to the practical questions which arise or may arise when a man feels aggrieved and thinks of seeking redress. Persons between whom there is a dispute; a thing which is the subject of dispute; some form of action for resolving the dispute by process of law: these are the common elements of litigation between parties. This evidently does not apply to crimes, or to all private wrongs; but the application is quite wide enough to support a classification which in truth is only a rough one. Do the persons concerned fall under any rules of law limiting or specially modifying their capacity or liability? What rights are recognised by law with regard to the subject-matter in question? Can it be owned, or exclusively enjoyed? One of the parties, perhaps, claims by sale or bequest: could the thing be given by will? could the sale invest him with the rights he claims to exercise? What, on the whole, is the resulting duty or liability? Then, supposing the rights of the parties to be settled, what are the available remedies? What is the active form, so to speak, of the legal result? or in English legal phrase, what is the cause of action? Can compensation be recovered in money, or is there any other, and what form of redress?

Persons are *prima facie* equal in modern, but not in ancient, law.

The distinction between law relating to persons and law relating to things may seem to the modern reader, perhaps, not to be a real one, or not one of the first importance. For things (whatever we include in the conception of a thing, which we are not yet considering) can plainly have no place in legal rules except in connection with the duties and rights of persons. The material world as such is absolutely irrelevant to jurisprudence. Every rule of law must to this extent have to do with persons. And in modern Western law we find that one person is very like another, and differences between persons tend to be reduced to a minimum. In fact we can nowadays be tempted to regard the law of persons as identical with the law of family relations, in which the irreducible differences of persons, as we may call them, resulting from the conditions of sex and age, are of necessity most prominent. But in archaic societies it is not at all to be assumed that persons are alike. Nowadays we presume every man to have the full legal rights of a citizen in the absence of apparent reason to the contrary. If any man is not capable of buying and selling, suing and being sued, in his own name and on his own responsibility, there must be something exceptional about him. Undischarged bankrupts, for example, are not a very large proportion of our adult population. But at Rome in the time of Cicero or even of the Antonines a prudent man could not presume anything about a stranger's legal capacities. A person of respectable appearance who spoke Latin was not necessarily even free. We know that serious doubt whether a man was free or not was quite possible. If he was a slave, he had no legal rights; he was not a person at all in the eye of the law. If he was free, he might still be a freedman, or a foreigner (not to speak of minuter distinctions). If he was a Roman citizen he might still have a father living, and be under that father's power; again, he might have been emancipated or adopted. He might belong, in short, to any one of several conditions of men, each having its distinct and proper measure of legal capacities. For a Roman of the Republic, and even of the Empire down to Justinian's time and later, the question, "With what kind of person have I to do?" had a very clear and prominent legal meaning, and no question could be more practical.

Modern authors have not arrived at any general agreement either as to the precise meaning of the law relating to persons in the Roman classification (if indeed the meaning ever was precise), or as to what topics are conveniently included under such a head at the present day. There is however a general tendency to regard the law of persons as supplementary to the general body of legal rules. We are apt to ask first, not what are the respective capacities of the parties in the matter in hand, but what are the rights of the matter assuming all parties to be of full ability. Then we consider, as a possible accident in the case, whether any one is under any disability, or to any extent exempt from responsibility, by reason of some special personal condition. In books meant for practical use this method is commonly followed, the disabilities and immunities of infants, married women, and so forth, being explained with reference to the department of law or class of transactions which is the subject of exposition.

Exposition under General and Special Parts.

Another principle of division frankly based on convenience of exposition is that by which, in dealing either with a whole body of law or with a substantial department thereof, those principles and rules which are found in all or most portions of the subject, so that they may be said to run through it, are disposed of before the several branches are entered upon. Such principles and rules may relate to the nature of duties and rights in themselves, to the conditions of their origin, transmission, and extinction (*title*, as we have already used the word), or to the remedies applicable. The setting forth of these matters in advance, so as to avoid repetitions and awkward digressions in the subsequent detailed treatment, is called, after the modern German usage, the General Part of the work in hand. In the

Special Part the several topics are dealt with in order, and, the general principles having already been stated, only those rules are discussed which are peculiar to the subdivision in hand, or are in some peculiar way modified in their application to its contents. Thus Savigny's great work on Roman law is only the "General Part" of his projected system. Well framed legislative acts on large subjects usually proceed in some such manner from the general to the special. Thus the Indian Penal Code has chapters of "General Explanations," "Punishments," and "General Exceptions" (that is, the causes for which acts otherwise criminal are justified or excused), which come before the definitions of particular offences. The "preliminary" part of Sir James Stephen's *Digest of the* (English) *Criminal Law* is a well marked General Part. Again the first six chapters of the Indian Contract Act contain what a Continental writer would call the General Part of the law of contract, namely, rules of law by which the formation, validity, and effect of all kinds of contracts alike are governed in British India. The other chapters, which deal with sale, agency, and other species of contracts, might be called the Special Part of the Act. Notwithstanding the obvious advantages of this method, it has only gradually and of late years come into use among English lawyers; I do not say in name, which is of little moment, but in substance. The late Mr. Leake's excellent and accurate *Digest of the Principles of the Law of Contracts* is, however, a complete and systematic General Part for that subject. Where a wide field has to be covered, the method may well be applied on a smaller scale to subdivisions within the general scheme. It is hardly needful to remark that it is by no means necessarily confined to legal exposition; but it is specially appropriate for legal writings, including legislation, by reason of the number of technical ideas and rules of various degrees of generality which, in working out any topic, have to be constantly assumed as within the reader's knowledge.

CHAPTER V

PERSONS

LAW necessarily deals with duties and rights of persons. Those duties and rights are determined by the relations of persons to each other, depending partly on their acts and partly on events independent of them, and connecting those persons either immediately or through the medium of what we may call, provisionally and vaguely, the possible objects of common or conflicting interest. Using "things" as a compendious equivalent for this last phrase, we may say that persons are brought, by the operation of acts and events, into relations with things and with one another: that is to say, relations capable of begetting duties, rights, and claims; for the science of law regards none others. Claims are satisfied by Remedies, the various forms of legal redress: and the benefit of the appropriate

Relation of persons to things.

remedy, the "fruits of judgment" as we often say, is meted out according to the rules of Procedure. From this point of view we get another way of looking at the division of law as relating to Persons, Things, and Actions which we lately noticed. It is not proposed however to consider here whether this, or something like it, may have been in the mind of the Roman lawyers, though they did not distinguish the general ideas from the special forms assumed by them in the law of Rome. We shall proceed in our own fashion to use this clue for the better apprehension of some of the leading ideas of jurisprudence. It seems a convenient course to start from the following questions as being necessary and elementary. Who and what are the subjects[1] of duties? and how brought into relation with the possible matter of duties? Of what does that matter consist? How are the data for determining the existence of duties ascertained; and, when ascertained, how are the duties enforced? Further, there is after all these a question of great practical importance, namely: In what forms is the law made known? This last one, however, does not seem to admit of any

[1] The word is here used, of course, in the logical, not the political sense.

answer in general terms that can be of much practical benefit: and we shall deal with it apart, and with special reference to the authorities of the Common Law, in the second part of this work. In like manner it is not assumed that the other questions all stand on the same line in this regard. Rules of evidence and procedure are largely determined by national and historical conditions which, though not really arbitrary, cannot be accounted for by universal principles.

What is a Person?

First then we have to inquire, not what were the capacities of persons in Roman law, or what they are in English law, but what a person is; that is, what are the necessary marks of a person in law. Duties and rights belong to persons. Persons are the subjects of rights and duties: and, as the subject of a right, a person is the object of the correlative duty, and conversely. The subject of a right has been called by Professor Holland the person of inherence, the subject of a duty the person of incidence. "Entitled" and "bound" are the terms in common use in English, and for most purposes they seem adequate. Every full citizen is a person: other human beings, namely subjects who are not citizens, may be persons. But not every human being is necessarily a person, for a person is capable of rights and duties, and there may well be human beings having no legal rights, as was the case with slaves in ancient law.[1] Doubtless any such institution is repugnant to the spirit of modern laws, and, since the abolition of slavery in America, we can hardly find an example in Western civilised countries: but we are now examining what is conceivable and possible, not what is desirable or now prevalent. A person is such, not because he is human, but because rights and duties are ascribed to him. The person is the legal subject or substance of which rights and duties are attributes. An individual human being, considered as having such attributes, is what lawyers call a *natural* person.

Natural and artificial persons.

Is not a person, then, simply a human being considered as capable of rights and duties? No, for there are persons in law which are not individual human beings. Not only man is social, but within a society men act collectively, presenting a solid front, so to speak, to society at large. Groups, permanent or temporary, behave as individuals. There arise in this manner collective capacities and responsibilities which the law personifies for con-

[1] The Roman lawyers did sometimes, but rarely, use *persona* so as to include slaves: Gai. i. § 48, followed by I. i. 8, see Moyle's *Inst.* p. 87, 2nd. ed.

venience. We have artificial persons, or, as we say in the Common Law, corporations. Not that it is an affair of mere convenience. It would seem that in the history of institutions collective rights and responsibilities were antecedent to those of the individual: and under archaic systems of law, as in Hindu and to some extent in Slavonic society, we can still find the individual hardly disengaged from the bonds of the family. However that may be, we constantly need in modern law the conception of an *artificial person*, a subject of duties and rights which is represented by one or more natural persons (generally, not necessarily, by more than one), but does not coincide with them. It has a continuous legal existence not necessarily depending on any natural life; this legal continuity answers to some real continuity of public functions, or of special purposes recognised as having public utility, or of some lawful common interest of the natural persons concerned.[1]

The action of an artificial person, be it observed, is not a merely legal or technical one. We make use of it every day for the common purposes of

[1] It would be extremely interesting to trace the history of the Roman idea of *universitas* and of its revival in European and English mediæval law. Such a task is of course beyond the scope of the present undertaking.

life, and in applications going far beyond those which courts of justice admit. We ascribe a single will and responsibility to the Ministry of the day, to voluntary associations and (what perhaps is most curious of all) to a newspaper. In some cases the artificial person of common speech may be, or may approximately coincide with, an artificial person in law too. Thus in England a newspaper may possibly belong (and nowadays often does) to a company incorporated under the Companies Acts; and railway companies are without exception, I believe, corporations. In other cases, as that of the Ministry, there can be no question of collective legal personality. But we never trouble ourselves, for extra-legal purposes, to think of this.

Nations personified.

In political discourse we so constantly personify nations that we almost forget the artificial character of our language: and yet the unrestrained use of metaphor in politics is quite capable of grave consequences. The essential truth involved in speaking of France or the United States as a person is that the governors of a civilised nation expect the nation to have the benefit of engagements made with their predecessors, and in turn are expected by the governments of other nations to answer for the public acts of their predecessors as well as for their own. Without the corporate idea of "perpetual succession" and continuous responsibility there could be no stability or confidence in dealings between nations. Whatever goes beyond this may run into dangerous fancies; as when the results of social and economic conditions in the foreign enterprises, say of Russians or Englishmen, are set down to a national passion of enmity, or design of deliberate ambition, like those with which we are familiar in individuals. To charge or credit "France" or "Austria" with particular habits or dispositions is, at best, to make a statement about the traditions of policy which are known by experience to prevail in the public affairs of that country: at worst it is to make wide assertions about the collective character of a multitude of people, including many and diverse types, and far too numerous for any one man to be even superficially acquainted with at first hand. Sometimes countries and populations are personified in this manner which contain internal elements of extreme diversity, and have not or have never had any true national unity; as, on a great scale, India, and, on a smaller one, Ireland. In such a case the metaphor is a degree more remote, and the danger of fallacy (commonly by taking some part or parts for the whole) is greater. But these matters lie beyond the province of law.

Corporations.

In the Common Law we call artificial persons corporations. Their existence is necessary to avoid the tedious and cumbrous processes which would otherwise be required for the carrying on of joint undertakings in which a large number of citizens are or may be interested. It is a natural following out of the same reasons to limit by law, as is done in England, the number of persons who may carry on business jointly without incorporation.

Firms.

We have in an ordinary partnership firm an example of artificial personality lying just on the borders of social or commercial convention and law. The firm is a person by mercantile usage: it is always and everywhere treated in business accounts, correspondence, and so forth, as a person distinct from the individual partners. In English-speaking countries it is quite common for a firm to go on using a name which has long ceased to be borne by any individual partner; though elsewhere this is not generally allowed. As to making the firm a person, legal usage is not uniform. In Scottish law, and, I believe, on the Continent of Europe generally the firm is recognised as a person: in the Common Law it is not. In classical Roman law we are hardly within sight of such a question, for the prevailing idea is still the management of common property, and the idea of joint interest in a joint enterprise is only beginning to emerge.

The State.

The greatest of artificial persons, politically speaking, is the State. But it depends on the legal institutions and forms of every commonwealth whether and how far the State or its titular head is officially treated as an artificial person. In England we now say that the Crown is a corporation: it was certainly not so when the king's peace died with him, and "every man that could forthwith robbed another."[1]

Legal capacities.

We have next to speak of the legal capacities of persons. They tend to equality in modern systems, as we said above,[2] but some inequality remains and must remain.

Of natural persons: physical disabilities.

First as to natural persons. There are physical conditions necessarily affecting the powers of the individual to manage and be answerable for his own affairs. Normally, we all have to pass through tender age and adolescence, or, in the Common Law term for the whole period before full age, infancy. When a man or woman is

[1] A. S. Chron. *anno* 1135. [2] P. 100.

of full age must be ascertained by the positive rules of the system of law in question. The prescribed age has varied in different systems from eighteen years (or, exceptionally, less) to twenty-five, which I think is the superior extreme. The Common Law term of twenty-one years is a reasonable mean. Full age may be fixed at different periods for different purposes: thus ability to marry without the consent of one's parents, if living, may be postponed (as it is in France) to a later age than general ability to manage one's affairs. Abnormally, people may be disabled by insanity at any age; the ascertainment of insanity, its effects in excluding responsibility, and the administrative measures necessary or proper for preserving the property of insane persons and checking abuses, have to be provided for by every system of law in its own way. So far as general principles are involved they belong mainly to public law.

Causes of variation in sex and family relations.

Another class of personal distinctions rests on the constitution of the family. Such distinctions are, in part, ultimately grounded on the physical difference of sex, and on moral differences assumed by the law to accompany it. In private law married women undergo some loss of legal capacity in all or almost all systems of law,[1] while in some systems all women are or have been under disabilities. In public law, and in every known system so far as public law goes, all women are under some disabilities and are exempt from some duties, that of military service for example, where it exists as a general duty of citizens. We find, on the other hand, variations of personal capacity derived from family relations which belong only to some particular type or stage of family institutions. The subjection of adults to paternal power among Roman citizens, the limited capacities of a member of a Hindu "joint family," may be taken as examples.

Special disqualifications, penal or otherwise

Further, there are special personal disqualifications or diminutions of legal capacity in every system of law. Some of these have a penal character, or at least savour of preventive and compulsory discipline: such are the disabilities of convicts, bankrupts, and (in some systems) declared spendthrifts. Others are attached to certain public offices or positions for reasons of

[1] The prohibition of bigamy, which applies to married men as well as women in modern law, has never been reckoned as a point of legal incapacity; by marriage the original capacity is not destroyed but fulfilled. So no one would say that a sitting member of Parliament had lost his capacity of being elected.

policy not dishonourable to the individual. Such are in England the disqualifications of clergymen, and of persons holding various offices, to sit in Parliament. In modern law these disqualifications (or exemptions, which no less occur) are almost or wholly confined to public law.[1] But in the Middle Ages a man could renounce his whole legal personality, public and private, become as it was called "civilly dead," by entering one of the regular orders of religion, and this may possibly be so still in some of the jurisdictions where the Roman Catholic religion is exclusively or principally recognised by the State, and its monastic and other societies of professed religious persons have an official standing. We are not aware that the institution survives in any of the greater States of Europe.

Artificial persons: their in capacities different from those of natural persons.

Passing to artificial persons we find that their capacities are not subject to most of the causes of variation which affect those of natural persons. Obviously a corporation cannot be an infant or insane. It may be insolvent; it is the common experience of our own time that, as an idle rhymer

[1] This would seem to be the grain of truth in the strange view taken by those writers who have rejected the distinction between Public and Private Law, and treated Public Law as a branch of the Law of Persons.

once wrote, "winding-up cometh to limited things." For reasons of practical convenience, however, insolvent corporations are, in England at any rate, dealt with by special forms of procedure differing from those used in cases of individual bankruptcy. Corporate capacity, on the other hand, is subject by its nature to restraining conditions from which the acts of natural persons are free.

Limitation by need of agency.

First, an artificial person can act only by means of some natural person or persons having authority to represent it, "actorem sive syndicum" as the Romans said; a railway company must act through its board of directors, and the like. Hence a corporation can do nothing which cannot be done by an agent. The full importance of this cannot be shown here, for the exposition would have to assume some detailed knowledge of law. But it is a matter of universal principle that there can be no real agency to do an obviously unlawful act. Hence follows a restriction on corporate responsibility which must be specially noted.

Corporations, how far liable for wrongs.

Secondly, then, a corporation cannot commit crimes, for it cannot authorise them. If the members or representatives of a corporation affected to authorise a criminal act in its name, they would merely make themselves liable as individuals.

To put an extreme case, if the East India Company had rebelled against the Crown, not the Company but the directors would have been guilty of high treason. But a corporation may have positive duties imposed on it by public law, and may incur penalties (though not criminal punishment in the strict sense) by failure or neglect in that respect. Such duties may be directly imposed on a corporation in connection with the special purposes for which it is constituted, or as an equivalent for privileges granted by the State; or the corporation may incur them by carrying on a trade or business to which they are attached by the general law. Further, a corporation may be liable for civil wrongs committed by its agents in the course of their employment, just as a natural person may be; and on principle there appears to be no reason why, consistently with the general idea of artificial personality, it should not be liable to the same extent. This is certainly the doctrine of the Common Law, though in some points it is not yet wholly settled in England.

Thirdly, many corporations are created expressly for special purposes, and their powers are limited to the execution of those purposes, and what is reasonably incident thereto. This is the case with most corporations in modern times, and there has even been a tendency to suppose the principle universal. Practically such cases almost always fall under some special legislative rule: but the interpretation of such rules has been doubtful enough to leave room for controversies of principle.

A corporation has distinct rights and duties not only as against persons outside it, but as against its own members. They can be its creditors or debtors. On the other hand its debts and claims against other persons are not the same as theirs. "Si quis universitati debetur, singulis non debetur, nec quod debet universitas singuli debent."[1] This is a necessary consequence of the corporation being a distinct person in law. How far the individual members can derive profit from corporate property or business, or be liable to contribute to the payment of corporate debts, has to be determined by the particular system of law and the constitution of the particular corporation. The formation of corporations, again, is a matter of positive regulation; though it may be taken as a principle of general jurisprudence that the authority of the State is requisite. Such authority may be conferred once for all, as regards a class of corporations, by general

Corporate duties and rights: formation of corporations.

[1] Ulpian, D. 3, 4, quod cuiuscunque universitatis, 7, § 1.

Corporeal things.

The kind of "things" with which we are most familiar are material sensible objects which can be dealt with in the way of manual use. No difficulty occurs in treating a house, a book, or a sheep, as things. As borrower of a book, I have the right of keeping the book for the agreed time, or until re-demanded, and the duty of returning it. The book is plainly not the same as my rights, or any one's, regarding the book, or the sum of all possible rights. It would still be a real book if it belonged to nobody. We are not now considering what the possible rights, of ownership or otherwise, may be. We take it provisionally as common knowledge that an owner who has not parted with any of his rights has large powers of use and disposal over the thing owned, powers which are indefinite even though they may be limited in certain directions by rules of law.

Aggregates.

There is no trouble, again, in extending this notion of a "thing" to an aggregate of material things, such as land with a house and other buildings on it, a library with all the books in it, a flock of sheep. Any of these aggregates may be treated as a single thing if we find it convenient. Physical continuity is in no way essential to the identity and singleness of the rights existing over material objects.

Physical discontinuity makes it, no doubt, easier to separate those rights and form new combinations; but easier only in degree. One sheep may be bought and driven off from the flock; one chair out of a set may be sold or given away. But also when the sheep becomes mutton each leg of mutton may have a separate owner; and a chimney in a house may be repaired and the old materials taken by the builder in part payment, or a whole wing of the house may be rebuilt and the materials sold in lots.

So far we have spoken of things (as Littleton said) whereof a man may have a manual occupation, possession, or receipt.[1]

Intangible elements of wealth.

But many elements of wealth are not tangible, as we know without assuming any special knowledge of law. The worth of five sovereigns is in the gold; the worth of a five-pound note, and the reason why we can get five sovereigns for it, is in the credit of the Bank of England. Whatever debts are owed to an individual, a firm, or a corporation in the course of business are part of the assets of the business. Nay more, the goodwill of a business, which is merely the right to go on using the old name, coupled with the expectation

[1] Litt. § 10.

that custom will still follow the name, is often of great pecuniary value.

Then we have exclusive rights which, though not merely personal, are only remotely connected with any tangible thing, and consist in the legal power of excluding others from competition in respect of their subject-matter. One may have an exclusive right to take fish in a certain piece of water, to ferry passengers across a river for hire at a certain place, to make and sell a new machine or instrument, to multiply and sell copies of a book or a print. Again we may have rights over tangible things which belong to others; rights of way over land, rights of using or detaining goods by way of loan, hire, or pledge, and others. These rights can be and are regarded in law as having distinct and measurable values, and whatever has such value is a thing, though not a bodily and sensible thing. These benefits can be part of a man's inheritance or goods, of his "estate and effects," to use the largest term known to our law; they are capable of transmission and, for the most part, of voluntary alienation. We must recognise as things, in fact, all objects of exchange and commerce which are recognised by the usage of mankind.

It is often said that such things have no being

Not merely creatures of law.

save in contemplation of law: the Roman phrase is "in iure consistunt." But this (although it contains a truth, as we may see hereafter) is not accurate as a general statement. There may be "groups of advantages," to use Professor Holland's happy term, which have an appreciable value though the law does not recognise them. Imperfect rights of the nature of copyright, for example, might exist outside the law by usage and courtesy. Such rights did in fact exist in the United States to a certain extent before the Copyright Act of 1891, as regards English books made over to American publishers; and they had a certain value to the American publisher, and consequently to the British author, although they were wholly unprotected by law, and (as events showed) precarious in fact. The goodwill of a business, again, would still have a commercial value if it were less efficiently protected by law than it is; and it would probably by no means lose the whole of its value even if it were not protected at all. The law began to protect it when it became notoriously valuable and not before. Hence it seems that in the case of incorporeal things the advantage or "group of advantages" enjoyed or to be enjoyed in fact is the true subject-matter of the right, and corresponds to the tangible object which we call a corporeal thing as distinct from the rights exercised over it. Of course the value of an incorporeal thing may be largely due to its recognition and protection by the law, and some incorporeal things may be called creatures of the law. But no one will suppose that the value of tangible property would not also be diminished if the law should cease to punish theft, or to decide questions of title. The parallel therefore seems to hold good notwithstanding the possible anomalies of extreme cases.

The legal nature of corporeal things.

At this point it may be worth considering, at the risk of an apparent paradox, whether corporeal things themselves are so corporeal as we think at first. For a material object is really nothing to the law, whatever it may be to science or philosophy, save as an occasion of use or enjoyment to man, or as an instrument in human acts. In fact there are parcels of terrestrial matter which are not things in the law. Of some such parcels, on grounds of necessary convenience, we have to say "communia sunt omnium," the water of the high seas for example; of other such we say, for reasons of religion or state, "nullius in bonis sunt." This is much easier to illustrate from the Roman law than from our own; for the Common Law abhors a vacuum of property:[1] a statement which the reader, unless he be already learned in the law, must provisionally take for granted. A thing which belongs to nobody is of no legal importance until something happens to bring a person into relation with it, and make it the subject-matter of enforceable rights. An old iron pot thrown away and dropped at the bottom of a canal, for example, might well be no more to the law than if it were in another planet. If it is something to the law, it is because the local law may happen to provide, as ours does, that abandonment shall not wholly destroy or suspend the legal qualities of a chattel which has once been a thing of value. So that on the whole perhaps we have good ground for saying that the "thing" of legal contemplation, even when we have to do with a material object, is not precisely the object as we find it in common experience, but rather the entirety of its possible legal relations to persons. We say entirety, not sum, because the capacity of being conceived as a distinct whole is a necessary attribute of an individual thing.

[1] Holmes, *The Common Law*, p. 237.

What the relations of a person to a thing can be must depend in fact on the nature of the thing as continuous or discontinuous, corporeal or incorporeal, and in law on the character and the extent of the powers of use and disposal which particular systems of law may recognise. A man who has copyright in a book can alienate but cannot destroy the copyright, though he may choose, on some scruple of conscience against monopoly in spiritual benefit,[1] not to exercise his right or reap the profit of it. The owner of an unique manuscript can destroy it in fact, but the law might conceivably forbid him to do so, and probably would if the obvious interest of those to whom things of unique value belong were not thought to be sufficient security against wanton destruction. Land, though it can be wasted or, in some situations, flooded, cannot be destroyed in the same sense as ordinary chattels; and some few chattels, such as the harder kinds of gems, may be considered indestructible, so far as ordinary accidents are concerned, as compared with perishable goods and even with relatively lasting materials of common use. Through all the range of natural

[1] Count Lyof Tolstoi not long ago disclaimed all interest in the copyright of his works for some such reason.

and legal diversities, however, a thing remains, for the lawyer's purposes, that which is attributed by law to the natural or conventional thing in regard to the rights and duties of persons.

Things as the potentiality of rights.

Here, then, we seem to have a necessary point of contact between law and philosophy. The lawyer as well as the metaphysician is driven, when he takes to thorough-going analysis, to face idealism. What we commonly call things are resolved by philosophical analysis into possibilities or occasions of perception. The idealist boldly says that the *esse* of material things is *percipi*. So we may say that in contemplation of law the *esse* of things is *haberi* or *in bonis esse*. That only is a thing which can, in the widest sense, be owned: it must be the subject-matter of rights that the law will recognise. An ownerless thing is for the lawyer pretty much what a "thing in itself" is for the philosopher. A *res nullius* is as void of legally intelligible contents as is a *Ding an sich* of intelligible contents of any kind. It is merely negative and irrational; the very notion of it excludes it from the world of rational import. We can see in it, at most, the potency of a future legal significance. The "books in my closet," in Berkeley's famous example, are merely the potentiality of the books I shall see when I open the closet. And so the ownerless abandoned thing, in systems which admit the extinction of property, is the mere potentiality of possession or ownership to come, whether the thing itself be buried treasure or a worthless tin pot. There is a legal vacuum till the act of an occupier or finder restores the thing, so to speak, to the world of legal reality. Hence, if we find in a particular system of law rules which are astute even to refinement to prevent this state of vacuum, there is no reason to treat such an endeavour as absurd. In fact the old masters of the Common Law did take the line of abhorring vacant possession or property, and put forth extreme ingenuity to avoid admitting it. "The law must needs reduce the properties of all goods to some man."[1] Without contending that they were consciously led by any philosophic reason, one may be allowed to think that, whether by scientific instinct or by good fortune, they showed themselves on this point at least as good philosophers as the Roman lawyers.

Summary. For the present purpose it is enough to know that in any case the legal notion of a thing must extend far beyond those objects which are "things"

[1] Doct. and Stud. dial. ii. c. 51.

in the popular sense as being capable of physical apprehension and use. Artificial aggregates of material objects, like a library or a flock of sheep, are only the first step in the extension. We have to include all distinct elements of wealth, though not tangible or sensible, which can be the source of profitable use or benefit to any certain person. The copyright, say of Jowett's *Plato*, is as much a thing as a bound volume of the book; railway shares are as much things as the rolling stock of the line.

How a particular thing can be used and enjoyed is a matter of fact conditioned by its nature and qualities, and this whether the thing be corporeal or incorporeal, save that an incorporeal thing may consist merely in the power or right of having some strictly limited advantage, using a particular path for example, while the possessor of a corporeal thing has indefinite though not infinite ways of manifesting his control over it. Questions may arise as to what forms of use, and how much use, the law will recognise as proof of effective and exclusive control. The use and enjoyment remain in themselves matters of pure fact. But we can speak with certainty of the rights of a possessor or owner only when we know what powers of use and disposal are recognised by the law; not only how things can be used, but how they may be, and how they may or must not be.

Events and acts.

Things are brought into relation with Persons by Events and Acts, which are in the world of law that which motion is in the world of matter. A great number, indeed the far greater number of events and acts are obviously of no legal import whatever. The falling of an apple from a man's own tree on his own ground makes no difference in any one's rights; and for the owner, if he is on the spot, to pick it up or not to pick it up, to eat or not to eat it, is an exercise of his lawful discretion which from a legal point of view is equally indifferent. But it is impossible to say of almost any event or act that it cannot have legal importance. A very small change of circumstances will make all the difference in this respect. Let that apple fall from a branch projecting a few feet beyond the owner's boundary, and come to rest on a neighbour's land. Here is matter for questioning at once. Whose is the apple now? Does it still belong to the owner of the tree? If so, may he go on his neighbour's land to take it, or must he ask for it? Or does it belong to the neighbour on whose land it has fallen? if so, unconditionally or subject to any and what conditions as to compensating the former owner? If a trespasser comes and takes the apple, whom has he wronged? All these questions, mostly trifling in the particular case suggested, but representing points which in other cases may be capable of involving great interests, have to receive distinct consideration, and may be not only distinctly but differently answered in different systems of jurisprudence. Walking, again, is a necessary and most common act of all persons who have the use of their legs; and so long as a man's legs take him where he has a right to be it is indifferent to the law. That it may, on the other hand, involve trespass, though oftentimes a merely nominal and innocent trespass, is common experience to most people who have walked in the country without strictly confining themselves to high roads and beaten paths.

Distinction of acts from events.

Every act may be said to be, in a large sense, an event. But it is convenient to use the word "event" only for that which happens or at least may happen[1] in the course of nature without

[1] As to events which may or may not be produced by human action it is often immaterial for many purposes to consider whether in fact they were so or not. The rights which arise on a man's death afford one obvious example. It is hardly needful to add that for our purpose only those acts count as such which can be

being directly determined by human intervention. It is proper to note that in archaic systems of law the part played by acts, as compared with events, is far less than it becomes in modern systems. For in early times, or, to speak more exactly, in early stages of civilisation, the range accorded to individual will and discretion is but a narrow one. Disposal of property by will, for example, is a relatively modern institution, and unrestricted power so to dispose of it, for example to the exclusion of a surviving wife or children, is not found at this day in countries where the Roman law has set the rule in matters of inheritance. Now the death of a man holding valuable property is an event which must necessarily have some legal effect; for the lands or goods which remain must belong to some one, be it the State or one or more individual persons, natural or corporate. In a system where dispositions by last will are not recognised, the event of death at once calls into operation the fixed rules of law, whatever they may be, which determine the succession to the deceased person's estate. In a system where a certain share cannot be alienated by will from

referred to a human agent. Such facts as a horse running away, a dog biting a man, are not acts but merely events.

a man's children, the will of a man who dies leaving children, so far as it disposes of what he has power to dispose of, is an act which takes effect upon the event of his death. So far as he has not exercised his disposing powers, and so far as concerns the portion of his estate which he cannot dispose of, the rights of his successor or successors are determined by the rules of law. Where full powers of testamentary disposition exist, and an owner has exercised them as to the whole of his property, the event of his death calls his act of disposition into play, and has not, as regards what was comprised in that act, any other operation.[1] So far as he has not exercised his rights, the event of his death operates as in the cases before put.

"Acts of the law," and "acts in the law."

Where changes are worked in the legal rights and interests of persons by rules of law not dependent on the will of any party, this is often and conveniently said to be an "act of the law" as contrasted with an "act of parties," although the contrast is not logically quite exact. Rules

[1] We are now speaking only of succession under a will as an alternative to intestate succession. The devolution of property in which limited interests have been created may depend on previous acts of parties, or on rules of law, or partly on the one and partly on the other. It is sufficient and preferable, for the purpose in hand, to take the simplest example.

of law have to determine the legal results of acts and events alike. But in many transactions the rules leave a wide freedom to the parties of appointing at their own pleasure what the result shall be; the law makes itself, in fact, the instrument of their intentions, and in a manner stands aside. As the Twelve Tables said: "Cum nexum faciet mancipiumque, uti lingua nuncupassit ita ius esto."

The phrase "act *in* the law" may conveniently be used for an act of parties which is fitted and designed to have a distinct legal effect, and, although it occurs with a wider application, it seems desirable to restrict it to this meaning, for which we have not otherwise any compendious English expression.

We might also speak if we chose of "events in the law," meaning events producing some legal effect; but since jurisprudence takes notice of events only so far forth as they can have legal effect, it will almost always be superfluous to use any such phrase.

The arising of liability to suffer punishment, or to pay compensation or otherwise submit to civil redress, by reason of a merely wrongful act, is not commonly spoken of as an act of the law, though the liability and the corresponding right to redress are of course fixed by law as much as the accrual of a right of inheritance or the like. The reason is that the contrast between an act of the law and an act of parties is not here applicable. A merely wrongful act cannot be an act *in* the law.

Acts considered as voluntary or otherwise.

There is no need or occasion for us to enter here on the psychological definition of an act. It concerns us as lawyers to know not so much what philosophers will call an act as of what kinds of acts, and to what purpose, the law takes notice. Generally speaking, the law has regard only to such acts as are voluntary and manifest. This is a necessary consequence of the nature of legal justice. The judgment of law must not only be but appear just, and can deal only with that which is capable of proof. The secret counsels and resolves of a man's mind are voluntary, but not manifest; the movements of a man's limbs when he gesticulates in a troubled dream, or walks in his sleep, are manifest but not voluntary. Perhaps these last are not properly to be called acts at all; in any case they are not on the footing of normal acts. How far, if at all, they can be a source of liability to the apparent actor may be a question of no small difficulty; but in fact cases of this kind are of such infrequent occurrence[1] in the affairs of justice that it would be quite out of place to dwell upon them in a general survey of legal ideas and categories. As to acts of the mind which are not directly manifested in outward performance, the law will not generally take account of them, both because they cannot be certainly known, and because no certain result can be assigned to them. Bodily motions, on the other hand, may be executed under direct mechanical constraint, without or against the person's will, as if a man's hand should be forcibly guided to make a signature or mark. Such motions are not acts at all, and are mentioned here only because former writers have thought it needful or proper to mention them by way of abundant caution. It is enough for us to attend to voluntary acts as they are commonly known and understood.

Intention and motive.

In considering voluntary acts with regard to the agent's responsibility, it is usual to distinguish between intention and motive. Intention is the wish or desire accompanying an act, and having regard not only to the act itself, but to the consequence or consequences to be produced. Thus intention includes will, but also covers much more

[1] To the best of my knowledge there is not in the whole mass of English reported decisions any authority governing such cases.

than is commonly understood by that term. It is needless to draw the line for any purpose not strictly philosophical. Near and obvious consequences are for all common purposes reckoned part of the act itself, as we shall see more at large presently. Thus when I press the button of an electric door-bell, we say that I ring the bell; in other words the sounding of the bell is included in my act, though it really depends on conditions quite beyond my control, such as the electrical apparatus being in order. My intention extends to procuring the door to be opened, being admitted if my friends are at home, leaving a card or message if they are out, or otherwise as the nature of my errand may be.

Motive as specific desire inducing action.

Motive is, unhappily, a more ambiguous word.[1] Sometimes we mean by "motive" the desire for a particular result which induces a person to act in a manner fitted to bring about that result. We speak here only of those motives which are effectual. For possible grounds of action which are considered and rejected, and therefore do not enter into the determination of any act, are plainly beyond the scope of legal judgment. Now, so far as desire of

[1] Bentham was troubled by its multifariousness, *Principles of Morals and Legislation*, ch. x. § 1, ss. iv.-vi.

this or that particular result is concerned, it would seem that nothing can be present in a man's motives (that is, effectual motives) which is not also present in his intention. For his intention, however far it extends, is determined, point for point, by his desires. The desired and intended consequences of an action must be commensurate with the desires that prompted it. Every representation of a preferred object in contemplation has its active equivalent in the formed intention. In deliberation we work backwards from the ultimate object to the intermediate means, and end with the immediate act to be done: in will or intention we start from the immediate act and look forward to the desired consequences. This was clearly seen by Aristotle, who points out that the contents of deliberation (the weighing of motives) and choice (the formation of intention) are the same, except that in choice the matter of deliberation is finally determined; intention is the sum of what is chosen as desirable among the objects of desire:[1] the two processes are in reverse order, for in deliberation

[1] *βουλευτὸν δὲ καὶ προαιρετὸν τὸ αὐτό, πλὴν ἀφωρισμένον ἤδη τὸ προαιρετόν· τὸ γὰρ ἐκ τῆς βουλῆς προκριθὲν προαιρετόν ἐστιν. Eth. Nic.* III. iii. 17. Aristotle looks to the active process of the mind (*βούλησις, προαίρεσις*) where we look to the materials or result of the process (motive or desire, intention). It is not obvious that Aristotle's way is the worse.

we proceed from the ultimately desired end back to the means, until we come to the step we shall have to take to start the train of consequences, while in intention the actual order of the expected events is represented, proceeding from the step first taken through the consequences to the farthest result expected and desired.[1] A tradesman, for example, wishes to improve his business. He forms the design of taking a shop in a better quarter; and, as this involves doing all things necessary for that purpose, he comes down from the general idea to planning the details. In the execution he must work the other way, going through the series of acts to realise the main purpose. First, he sees or writes to an agent, then goes to view a vacant shop; then, if it suits him, negotiates for a lease, executes the lease, enters into possession, and trades at the new address. Finally, if his forecast is justified, he has the improved custom which he began by desiring. On the whole then a man cannot intend what he has not chosen, although he may be driven to choose, as the least of inevitable evils, a course which he dislikes in itself. The means to some desired end often have undesirable

[1] *Eth. Nic.* III. iii. 11, 12; I adopt Mr. Stewart's rendering of *τὸ πρῶτον αἴτιον* (Notes on the *Nic. Eth.*, Oxford, 1892). Cp. Sully, *Outlines of Psychology*, 2nd ed. 589.

features which are tolerated for the sake of the end. No voyage can be wholly free from perils of the sea; no traveller can explore a new country without known and unknown dangers; no great work of engineering can be executed without some risk to life and health.[1] Every one would make his work perfectly safe if he could, but the risk that remains after taking all reasonable and practicable precautions has to be accepted though not welcomed. There is a difference, again, between drawbacks which are a necessary part of a proposed course, and those which are only more or less probable incidents; in the former case an action repugnant in some ways is nevertheless decided upon, as where a well-grown tree is cut down for the sake of light or space; in the latter there is only the taking of adverse chances, as where a mountaineering party, rather than abandon an expedition, crosses a *couloir* liable to be swept by falling stones.

Motive as constant moral disposition.

So far we have taken motive in the sense of external motive, as it may be called, the particular inducement to a course of action. But "motive"

[1] *Qui veut la fin veut les moyens* is a general truth in this qualified sense: one might add as a gloss, *même quand il voudrait autre chose.*

can also mean internal motive,[1] the general moral quality or disposition of the agent which is a constant element as compared with particular inducements, and gives weight in his deliberation to this or that inducement. The effect of general moral quality or disposition in the process of deliberation and choice is for many purposes more important than the average or objective value (so far as there is any) of things reputed desirable. And this seems to be the meaning of "motive" preferred by the best modern authors when exact distinction is required. In ordinary language, when we speak of the motives for an action, we are for the most part consciously or unconsciously taking external and internal motives together. Internal motive, or the general disposition from which an act proceeds, is obviously not capable of proof by the facts of a particular case alone.

External motive is often considered in law.

If we are asked, therefore, how far the law regards motive as distinct from intention, we must answer with the counter-question: External or internal motive? There is no doubt that the law does take account of external motive as embodied in intention. Motive in this sense, the desire or

[1] All motive is internal in one sense, for it can operate only in consciousness. But it is enough that the distinction be intelligible.

purpose operative in the agent's choice, is often capable of proof, and may be material to show the intention with which an act was done: and in cases where the question is by whom an act was done, the presence or absence of motive—that is, the fact or probable appearance that a given person desired an end which the act was fitted to attain, or the absence of any such appearance—is constantly discussed, and may, in the absence of direct evidence, have great weight. In a case of unlawful wounding the prisoner's intent to do grievous harm may appear not only from the nature of the weapon, the circumstances of the attack, and the like, but from previous declarations of ill-will towards the person attacked. Similar considerations apply in cases where we have to consider whether there has been an intentional act of a given person at all. The first Lord St. Leonards was known to have made a will; the will was not forthcoming after his death; proof of its contents was however forthcoming, and was admitted. It had to be decided whether Lord St. Leonards had destroyed the will with the intention of revoking it, or, on the contrary, it had been secretly stolen; and it was shown that his conduct and expressed feelings, down to the last days of his life, had been those of a man who believed the will to be in existence and wished it to take effect. On this evidence the will was established.[1] A more familiar example of the same principle is the admission of evidence of good character in criminal cases.

Internal motive examinable only in exceptional cases.

Internal motive, on the other hand, is not a normal matter of judicial proof or condition of legal consequences in particular cases, though it may be taken into account by legislation, or by what is called the policy of the law on the one hand and judicial discretion on the other. Offences which commonly proceed from a depraved or dangerous moral habit may be liable on that account to more severe punishment; and lighter sentences will be passed (so far as consistent with the safety of society) on those who break the law not from greed, lust, or malice, but by some perversion of natural affection or benevolence. A man who steals food for his hungry children is a thief as well as one who steals money to buy liquor and get drunk, but they will hardly be punished alike under a system which leaves any discretion to the judge. The positive definitions and judgments of law, as distinct from judicial discretion, do not as a rule attempt to

[1] *Sugden* v. *Lord St. Leonards* (1876), 1 P.D. 154. Some of the very important matters involved are passed over as not relevant for the present illustration.

consider internal dispositions. Acts can be proved and their consequences traced; the springs of conduct are for the most part hidden. In some exceptional cases, however, the disposition from which an act proceeds is taken into account as distinct from the intention. The word "malice," when it means anything more than the intention of doing an unlawful act, seems to be the specific mark of such cases in the language of the Common Law.[1]

Complexity of intention.

It has already appeared in the course of the foregoing explanation that intention is almost always manifold and complex. Most acts are done with a view to a series of results, of which some or one are generally subordinate to some other result or group of results for the sake of which the action is undertaken, and which is commonly called its end or purpose. A man writes with the proximate intent of setting down certain words and sentences; if he is writing a book, he has the further intent that they may be printed and published, and his ultimate and principal ends may be to instruct or amuse those who read the book, to procure gain or

[1] There is no doubt, I think, that malicious prosecution and some other analogous wrongs do form an exceptional class of this kind. In recent times the tendency has been rather to extend than to narrow it.

reputation to himself, to advance the interests of his party or to promote some undertaking which he has at heart, or all or some of these things may be desired by him in equal or various degrees. A householder is aroused in the night by the sound of footsteps which he believes to be a robber's, and fires a shot out of the window. His immediate intent is to discharge the gun or pistol. His further intent is to scare away the thief, and to summon to his aid any constable or other true man who may be within hearing; these are two consistent and simultaneous but distinct purposes.

Proximate consequences reckoned as part of act.

For simplicity's sake we commonly reckon the immediate and usual consequences of an act, when to all appearance they are intended and follow as intended, as part of the act itself, and we speak of intention only with reference to the farther consequences. In the act of shooting, for example, the man's own act stops, if we are to speak with strict precision, at pulling the trigger, but the discharge of the gun in the direction given to the barrel by the man's aim is counted as part of the act. This is well illustrated in an early passage of that curious and discursive book, Abraham Tucker's *Light of Nature.*

In speaking of action, besides the several co-existent

motions and several successive volitions before-mentioned, we ordinarily comprehend several operations of other agents acting in a series towards compleating the purpose we had in view, provided we conceive them necessarily consequent upon our volition. Thus when Roger shot the hawk hovering over his master's dove-house, he only pulled the trigger, the action of the spring drove down the flint, the action of the flint struck fire into the pan, the action of the fire set the powder in a blaze, that of the powder forced out the shot, that of the shot wounded the bird, and that of gravity brought her to the ground. But all this we ascribe to Roger, for we say he brought down the felon; and if we think the shot a nice one, applaud him for having done a clever feat. So likewise we claim the actions of other persons for our own, whenever we expect they will certainly follow as we shall direct. When Squire Peremptory distrained his tenant for rent, perhaps he did no more than write his orders in a letter, this his servant carried to the post, the postman conveyed it into the country, where it was delivered to the steward, who sent his clerk to make the distress. Yet we ascribe the whole to the Squire's own doing, for we say he distrained his tenant, and call it a prudent or a cruel act, according as we think of the circumstances of the case.

Hence the law maxim, he that does a thing by another, does it himself; which though valid in Westminster Hall will not hold good in the schools of metaphysics, for there we shall find nothing an act of the mind that is not the immediate product of her volition. But for the uses of prudence and morality we must recur back again to the common language, because we cannot judge of the merits of men's doings without taking the consequences into our idea of the action. Pulling a trigger or drawing characters upon paper, are neither good nor bad, right nor wrong, considered in themselves; but as the trigger so pulled shall occasion the slaughter of a man, or of some vermin, or only a bounce in the air; as the characters so drawn shall tend to the necessary security of our property, or to bring a hardship upon our neighbour, or shall carry no meaning at all, we pronounce the action prudent or idle, moral or wicked.[1]

Hence, as Tucker discerned more plainly than some later writers, it is useless for lawyers to consider voluntary acts as if they stopped at the surface of the human body, or to distinguish between will and intention by reference to nervous and muscular motions. We take the notion of Will as we find it in common-sense morality, resisting temptations to digress on the right hand into speculative ethics or on the left hand into psycho-physiology. So taking it, we can use the extension of will to natural and intended external consequences as a mere harmless convenience of language and of compendious thinking.

Remote consequences as connected with intention.

When we come to remoter consequences of acts they rapidly become complex, so that at first sight it is by no means clear which of them were intended or foreseen and which not, and then we may have to fall back on other evidence of what the person acting did at the outset intend and desire. A man comes out of

[1] The *Light of Nature Pursued*, ch. ii. *ad fin.*

his house carrying a stick; after walking a few steps he turns back, opens the door, goes in, and comes out again with an umbrella. We may guess that he returned to fetch an umbrella because he thought the sky looked rainy. But this is only one guess and may not be the right one. He may not have had any thought of being rained upon or any intention of protecting himself from rain. Perhaps he thought he would take the umbrella to be mended. Perhaps he went back for something quite different, and then took up the umbrella rather than the stick by distraction or mere accident. The connection of act and intent is already remote and precarious, even in so simple a case, unless we have some independent guidance for our judgment.

Archaic law disregards intention.

Even manifest intention is hardly treated as a possible or proper subject-matter of judicial proof in archaic systems of law. Where the analysis of general conceptions, if any there be, is of a crude and rudimentary kind, and the methods of proof are cumbrous and of inflexible formality, there are no means of apportioning liability for acts with regard to the actor's intent. Early law fastens on some particular external quality of an act, and makes that the decisive test. Thus in the modern

Common Law the difference between murder, the capital or more culpable degree of homicide, and manslaughter, the less culpable, involves not only the notion of intention but considerable refinements on it. But originally "murder" meant nothing but secret killing, especially by poison or witchcraft.

Unintended consequences and intent without consequences.

It is common knowledge that consequences of an act which are manifestly intended often do not follow, and unintended consequences do; as where one throws a cricket ball at the wicket, or a stone at some object chosen at random, and misses; where a soldier roused in camp by a night alarm seizes his pistol and, firing in haste, shoots his own toes instead of the supposed enemy; where a man trying to open a locked door with the proper key finds that the pipe of the key is choked or the lock is out of order, and the like. We must by no means suppose that ineffectual intentions are of no importance in law, for such intentions may well be the ground of liability for more than one reason. Attempts to commit offences are commonly punishable, and the menace of bodily violence in act is a complete civil injury by our law, though it may stop short of the actual application of force; or, as we say in technical language, assault without battery is actionable. The highest crime known to the law, that of high treason, is singularly enough defined in its first branch, namely, that of compassing or imagining the death of the king, his consort, or their son and heir-apparent, as consisting in intention; so that even complete execution of the design is only evidence of the intention which constitutes the offence. But this appears to be a historical curiosity of the law not fitted to illustrate any general principle.

Acts as creating duties.

We may now take a summary view of the ways in which acts can produce responsibility, in other words create duties and corresponding rights. A great number of acts are in themselves merely indifferent to the law, that is to say, do not work any change in existing duties or rights. We say "in themselves" because not every act which can be done with immediate impunity is rightful or approved, and the distinction between acts allowed as rightful and acts and conduct barely tolerated can be and is applied in the administration of justice in various indirect ways.

Acts involving intention or consent.

Acts which do create or modify rights do so either with or without the intention of the parties. If the legal consequences are designed and intended by the parties, the act is an act in the law in the sense before explained. In abnormal cases there may be the appearance of an act in the law without the reality, as where a party, by reason of fraud or otherwise, wholly misconceives the nature and proper effect of the act he purports to do. Particular transactions, again, may be forbidden or restrained by positive rules of law, so that acts disregarding those rules (a ceremony of marriage within the prohibited degrees, for example) have no legal effect. Many acts in the law require the concurrent intention of two or more parties, which is called consent. Consent must be both real and lawful for the act to be valid.

Imperfect consent.

Again, consent ought to be full and free; it is not enough that there is any sort of consent. Quite real consent may be brought about by compulsion or fraud, and the act, though not a nullity, may be liable to be deprived of its effect if disputed in the interest of the party who has been coerced or deceived. Similar rules apply, to some extent, to those acts where only the intention of one person is in question, of which dispositions by will are the most important. We do not enlarge on these matters, for we are now considering only what are the possible effects of acts, not examining the conditions that determine what effect particular kinds of acts are to have. But there is one distinction to be mentioned which is of great importance in almost every branch of private law.

Void and voidable acts.

An act that is incapable of taking effect according to its apparent purport is said to be void.[1] One which may take effect, but is liable to be deprived of effect at the option of some or one of the parties, is said to be voidable. A voidable act can be objected to only by the party specially entitled to dispute it, or some one standing in his place, and, so far and so long as no such objection has been made, it must be treated as valid and effectual. Moreover the power of objecting is limited in certain ways out of regard for the interests which other persons may have acquired in good faith on the strength of an apparently valid act. In this manner acts of disposal or consent which were not binding in the first instance as between the parties may be completely binding as between a party whose consent has been induced by fraud, or the like, and an innocent third person.

We must be careful not to say that a void act can have no legal effect at all. It cannot produce its intended or apparent effect, but it may have serious effects which were not intended. A

[1] It does not follow that an act void in its primary intention may not have some effect in some other capacity.

ceremony of marriage between two persons of whom one is already married to a living wife or husband is a nullity so far as concerns the pretended marriage, but it will generally constitute the offence of bigamy.

The law generally aims at giving effect, so far as possible, to the lawful acts and intentions of parties. But it is needful for security's and certainty's sake that intentions of altering existing rights and making dispositions for the future be sufficiently manifested, and, with this object in view, the laws of all countries require particular forms to be observed in particular kinds of acts. These requirements are not so much restraints upon individual freedom as safeguards for its full and deliberate exercise. To some extent, however, official records of acts may be ordained, and registration made directly or indirectly compulsory, in the paramount interest of the State. Among the possible objects of such regulation are the securing of duties payable to the public revenue, the supervision of the property and affairs of corporations, and the certainty and publicity of titles to property.

Formal conditions of validity.

Acts and events may produce liability without the intention of any party in various ways. Among such acts are, of course, crimes and active wrongs;

Liabilities not intended.

but involuntary liability has a much wider scope, for it likewise occurs in many cases where there is only a technical default or no default at all. A man to whom a payment is made by mistake incurs the duty of repaying the money, but he has done no wrong and has not broken any duty unless and until, on being informed of the facts, he refuses to repay. Persons in certain situations, again, have to answer for accidental damage caused by things under their control even if the accident was inevitable. Here there may be said to be a breach of duty, but only because the law, for special reasons,[1] has in these cases imposed an absolute and unqualified duty of preventing one's property from doing harm. Thus a man, if he keeps a wild animal, does so at his peril, and persons dealing with other things which are accounted especially dangerous are under the like rule. In the case of breach of contract the duty broken or not performed has been imposed on the party by his own consent and will, and therefore the question is generally not whether he was to blame, but only what he undertook and

[1] In many cases the historical origin of exceptional rules of law has very little to do with the reasons that can be assigned for upholding them in modern times. But where an archaic rule has continued in force to our own time without any serious opposition, we must presume that at least plausible modern reasons exist.

whether he failed; and if he did fail, from whatever cause, to fulfil his undertaking, he is liable. Here, however, the liability, although not exactly intended, was contemplated, and, in the event of failure to perform the promise, accepted beforehand.

Degrees of involuntary liability.

We may take these last mentioned classes of cases together, as differing much in other respects, but having this much in common, that the liability does not depend on any ethical judgment of the party's conduct. So taking them, we may reckon them as comprising the most positive and artificial grounds of liability. The next degree is where the party has come under some duty of using diligence, and has brought about damage to a fellow-citizen by falling short of the measure of diligence, "due care and caution" as it is often called, which the circumstances are deemed to require of a reasonable man. This ground of liability is what the Common Law calls Negligence and the Roman law Culpa. We have to develop and apply this idea partly in criminal law, and to some extent, though not in the first line, in the law of contract (since many kinds of contracts involve an undertaking to use due care and caution), but chiefly in the law of civil wrongs.

Then we have the cruder and simpler forms of wrong-doing where there is not merely failure in a positive duty, or culpable shortcoming, but a distinctly wrongful intention. Here the liability may be said to rest on obvious principles of natural as well as positive law. The common sense of justice would be shocked if the law did not give effect to it. Whether this shall be done in the region of civil or criminal law, or peradventure in both, can be determined only with regard to the civilisation and institutions of each particular commonwealth.

Liability for consequences.

It has been found a matter of no small difficulty, both in principle and in the application of the principles to particular cases as they occur, to determine how far a man shall be held answerable for the less obvious and direct consequences of his acts. Questions of this kind are referred by English-speaking lawyers to the head of "remoteness of damage." It is held that the actor, where he is liable at all, must answer consequences, whether intended or not, so far as they are "natural and probable," that is, according to the opinion now generally accepted and applied, so far as a reasonable man in his place and with his means of knowledge would have foreseen them. The subject can be profitably studied or expounded only by going into much more detail than would be convenient here.

CHAPTER VII

RELATION OF PERSONS TO THINGS: POSSESSION AND OWNERSHIP

General notion of property.

We have now surveyed in the rough the materials on which law has to work, that is to say, persons and things, and the medium by which they are brought into intelligible relations, that is to say, events and acts. The relations of persons to things in law have to be determined in accordance with the facts of life; and in daily life the importance of things is that they can be used and enjoyed. What we call the law of Property is, in the first place, the systematic expression of the degrees and forms of control, use, and enjoyment, that are recognised and protected by law. Possibly it may turn out to cover more, if we give the widest acceptable sense to the word Property; but it is this at the very least.

Control and enjoyment.

As a matter of fact, one may have the benefits of use and enjoyment in many degrees. So far as we take only the present into account, exclusive and effective control of a thing is the highest degree possible, for this includes power to deal with the thing, within the bounds of what its nature allows, at one's will and pleasure. In the notion of effectiveness we must include such continuance as will give time (though very little time may be enough) for the choice and execution of what shall be done. And we must further include some practical freedom in these respects. The man who fields a ball at cricket and instantly throws it up to the wicket has, for a second or two, control of the ball which is physically both exclusive and effective; but so soon as we look beyond the bare physical facts, we see that he has no use of it for himself and little or no discretion as to what he shall do with it, and does not think of having any. Nobody would think of saying that the ball belongs to him. He holds or detains the ball for a few moments, but not as his own or for his own benefit; to use the proper "word of art," as English lawyers say, he does not possess it. Different things are capable of very different kinds and degrees of physical control, and the question whether effective and exclusive control is shown in a particular case must be considered with regard to the qualities of the thing and the manner in which such things are habitually used and enjoyed. It may be a question of some difficulty. When it is so, the fault is not with the law but with the nature of things.

Enjoyment without control.

There are also many modes of enjoyment which are not exclusive, or not continuous, or partial in extent, or which fall short of general control in more than one of these ways. One may turn one's beasts out on a common; here the enjoyment is or may be continuous, but it is not exclusive. One may have the sole use of shooting or fishing over some other person's land or water; here the enjoyment is exclusive but not continuous. One may be accustomed to take water from a certain well in common with other persons; this is a benefit neither exclusive (save as to the use of the tackle during the actual operation of drawing water) nor continuous. One may be accustomed to pass and repass over a neighbour's land; this is a partial enjoyment of the uses of his land. It is not a continuous enjoyment by its own nature, and it is not exclusive if other persons or the neighbouring landowner himself also make use of the path. We have said nothing yet about legal rights. All this can be observed as matter of fact without considering what the law has to say to it, if anything. All these greater and lesser conveniences might exist with a certain amount of customary uniformity and even with a certain amount of practical security if there were no law of property at all. What the law has to do is to confirm and protect, so far as is thought proper, the relations of control, use, and enjoyment, which exist or may exist in fact. That a man who is peaceably enjoying land or goods shall not be disturbed by mere wanton greed or spite may be taken as an elementary need of society. What more the law can and should do may stand over. Possession—actual and peaceable use of things as one's own—must be protected to some extent.

Powers of disposition.

But this is not all. Present enjoyment and power of enjoyment are not the sum of man's power over things, either of what he has or of what he desires. Animals may generally not see beyond the present; savages may sometimes not look farther. Man, as a member of a family and a commonwealth, looks forward and outward.

He wants not only to use and enjoy, but to put or leave others in his place, and himself to take the place of others, in a regular and orderly manner. He must be able to traffic as a seller or as a buyer, to give or to receive bounty, to continue the name and wealth of his ancestors, to leave the world with the assurance that they may be continued in his posterity. For these ends law must do much. They might, even without law, not wholly fail to be compassed after some sort, but the result would be poor and precarious. And what the law must do is much more than the protection of existing occupation and enjoyment. Not only use but disposal is now in question; and we cannot protect the disposal of land and goods without regulating it. Conflicting claims have to be dealt with; we must have rules for knowing what dispositions are effectual, which among many claims are rights entitled to prevail.

We pass beyond the mere defence of possession, Title.
and we have to adjudge on which side is the better right to possess and enjoy the subject of dispute. It has to be considered not only whether a man has been deprived of possession, "disseised" in the language of the Common Law, but who is the right

heir, whether there has been a perfect sale, whether a will can stand. In one word, possession is a matter of fact, or at least founded in fact; whereas title, as the absolutely or relatively best right to a thing which may be in dispute, is matter of law, not only defined but created by law. The law may restrain powers of use; it must determine powers of disposal. When we get beyond actual control and occupation, the extent of our power over things is what the law declares it to be. "A man," as Littleton said, "*cannot* have a more large or greater estate of inheritance than fee simple."[1] This does not mean that having an estate to oneself and one's heirs is in the Common Law the technical expression of the utmost conceivable degree of disposing power. Littleton could not have meant this, in fact, for when he wrote these words a tenant in fee simple could not leave his land by will except in a few places where local custom allowed it. The words mean exactly what they say, namely, that the powers of use and disposal, such as they are, which are incident to an estate in fee simple are, as regards whatever can be the subject of freehold tenure, the highest known to the law.

Still more is this the case with regard to partial

[1] Litt. § 11.

Partial modes of enjoyment defined by law.

and limited modes of enjoyment. When a man claims to have the use of his neighbour's land in some way,—to ride across it, to get water from a well, to cut firewood, to dig gravel,—the first question is what rights of that kind the law will recognise. The measure and the value of such rights depend on their legal definition. We may say of them for this reason—not because they are incorporeal, which has already appeared not an adequate ground[1]—that "in iure consistunt." One step farther, and we come to claims, not of any direct use or profit to be had by one's own acts, but to restrain a neighbour from acts which, if done in the use of his own land or goods, would in some way diminish our use or enjoyment of what belongs to us. A claim not to have one's windows darkened by new building is a common example, and perhaps the most striking. Here everything depends on the rule; we do not know whether there can be any right or legal interest at all until we know whether occupation of a house is ever, and if so when and on what conditions, deemed to carry with it the power of objecting to have the windows darkened. The English rules as to "ancient lights" have, in fact, not been received in the United States

[1] P. 125 above.

generally, so that the law and practice of the two countries are quite different. Light, or the benefit of light, is in itself not a thing at all in the legal sense any more than it is matter in the sense of the physicist; and the question is how far the enjoyment, in some definite manner and measure, of that which in itself is common to all the world can or does give rise to definite rights to be free from interruption in such enjoyment.

Ownership. Ownership may be described as the entirety of the powers of use and disposal allowed by law. This implies that there is some power of disposal, and in modern times we should hardly be disposed to call a person an owner who had no such power.[1] If we found anywhere a system of law which did not recognise alienation by acts of parties at all, we should say not that the powers of an owner were very much restricted in that system, but that it did not recognise ownership. The term, however, is not strictly a technical one in the Common Law,[2]

[1] For this reason I cannot think it quite correct to say that "irresponsible possession, protected by a remedy availing against all others, makes ownership" (Williams, *Real Property*, 14th ed. p. 10). It does so if possession is a root of title; but that is a new and important condition.

[2] It occurs in modern Acts of Parliament, sometimes with the result of producing difficulties. See *Arrow Shipping Co.* v. *Tyne Commissioners*, 1894, A.C. 508. "*True* owner" has a distinct meaning.

we shall presently see why. We must not suppose that all the powers of an owner need be exerciseable at once and immediately; he may remain owner though he has parted with some of them for a time. He may for a time even part with his whole powers of use and enjoyment, and suspend his power of disposal, provided that he reserves, for himself or his successors, the right of ultimately reclaiming the thing and being restored to his power. This is the common case of hiring land, buildings, or goods. Again, the owner's powers may be limited in particular directions for an indefinite time by rights as permanent in their nature as ownership itself. Such is the case where the owner of Whiteacre has a right of way over his neighbour's field of Blackacre. As this example shows, what is thus subtracted from one owner's powers is generally added to another's. In short, the owner of a thing is not necessarily the person who at a given time has the whole power of use and disposal; very often there is no such person. We must look for the person having the residue of all such power when we have accounted for every detached and limited portion of it; and he will be the owner even if the immediate power of control and use is elsewhere. In the same way a political sovereign does not lose his independence merely because he has made a treaty by which he has agreed to forego or limit the exercise of his sovereign power in particular respects.[1]

Distinction of possession, ownership, real rights.

We are now in a position to take note of the manner in which ownership differs from possession on the one hand, and limited rights over particular things (*iura in re aliena*) on the other. Possession in fact—the effective and exclusive control of a thing—is prior to ownership and indeed to every legal rule and idea. The facts which we call actual or physical possession would still exist in a society where there was no recognition of individual property. But possession, as a fact, is interesting to lawyers only so far as legal results and incidents may attach to it;[2] and to give definite rights to a possessor because he is in possession is to admit individual rights of exclusive use and enjoyment. We say because he is in possession. A system of law which merely forbade personal violence might incidentally protect possession so far as any one who used actual violence in dispossessing another

[1] *Mighell* v. *Sultan of Johore*, 1894, 1 Q.B. 149, C.A.

[2] Cp. *Possession in the Common Law* (by Mr. Justice Wright and the present writer), p. 10, and see the first chapter of that book for detailed discussion.

might thereby render himself liable to a penalty or damages. This would not be saying anything of possession except that it was not a crime which deprived the possessor of his ordinary personal rights, or a condition in itself odious to the law. Still less does this involve any connection of possession with title. When possession as such is regarded as a proper subject of protection, that is to say, when dispossession without just cause (apart from any violence or physical damage incidental to the act) is treated as calling for a remedy, then the relation to ownership becomes apparent. If a person out of possession is to have a standing-point at all, possession must be capable of being wrongful as well as rightful. There must be rights to possess, or to be put in possession, that can be severed from present possession. There must be room for conflicting claims to possession, and rules for deciding which of two claimants has the better right to possess the thing in dispute.

Right to possess.

Now this brings us to very close quarters with ownership. For ownership, as the entirety of legal powers of use and disposal, must include, as the most important of those powers, in fact, as the one thing by which alone the rest can be made effective, the right to maintain or claim possession; a right which, though it may be suspended or deferred, cannot be wholly dissociated from an owner's relation to the thing owned.[1] Again, ownership is most commonly and completely manifested in actual possession and use. To deal with a thing at one's will is to deal with it like an owner; in the absence of manifest reason to the contrary, we suppose that a man is or claims to be owner of anything over which he exercises indefinite control. Thus active possession is a normal index of ownership (though by no means the only one even in common life), and the right to possess (whether immediate or not) is a necessary incident of ownership, or may perhaps rather be called ownership itself in its active or dynamic aspect. One who is out of possession and has a rightful claim to possess has need of the law's assistance. When he has recovered possession, he has not any need to ask the law to do more for him. Once in possession he can deal with his own in any lawful manner.

Value of possessory remedies to owners.

Hence it is commonly sufficient for an owner

[1] It may be, by reason of legal rules having lagged behind the facts of life and the convenience of mankind, that the facts are at last recognised only with the help of artifices or fictions. There may be nominal owners who cannot exercise any right of ownership for their own benefit. Separation of beneficial interest from legal title has occurred in both Roman and English law. But there is no need to dwell on this now.

to rely on his right to possession; and as it is commonly easier to prove the less right than the greater, not to speak for the present of the manner in which this works out in detail, it is often preferable to claim possession only. Nay more, it is possible for ownership to be sufficiently guarded for all practical purposes by a system of remedies which omits, or has come to omit, any such solemn and express form of asserting ownership as that to which the Romans emphatically gave the name of Vindication. In the Common Law this has actually happened. For some centuries all practical remedies for the recovery of both land and goods have been possessory, and property has meant, for judicial purposes, the right, or the best right, to possess. Conversely, that which a man was entitled to possess not only was correctly described by him in pleading as *res sua*, but could not be described in any other way.[1]

Possession as evidence of title.

But this leads us to a further development. Possession and use being the common outward signs of ownership, it is reasonable to presume, in the absence of proof to the contrary, that existing peaceable possession is rightful, and further to infer ownership from the right to possess which we have

[1] Holmes, *The Common Law*, p. 242.

thus presumed. Hence we treat the actual possessor not only as legal possessor but as owner, as against every one who cannot show a better right. As English lawyers say concerning interests in land, possession is *prima facie* evidence of seisin *in fee*: that is, not of legal possession or seisin alone, but of seisin coupled with the largest powers of use and disposal allowed by law. Then, if we regard the possessor as being rightfully in the exercise of control, we must allow him the powers of an owner within the limits of his apparent right. Not only his acts of use and occupation but his acts of disposal must be valid against every one who cannot make out a superior claim. And when the superior claim, if any such there be, ceases to be available, the rights founded on possession will be indistinguishable from the rights of ownership. In the case of movable goods which pass from hand to hand without formality this becomes obvious, for in that case possession is often not merely the natural and usual proof of ownership, but the only proof. We have come then to distinctly recognising possession as an origin of ownership, a "commencement of title" as our law calls it. Again we see that not only we have thus to recognise it, but a system of law can get on without recognising any other origin. Continuous possession is quite capable of being, not merely a possible foundation of ownership, but its only foundation and evidence. And this, once more, is exactly what has happened in the Common Law. With very few exceptions,[1] possession traced through a chain of lawful transfer, or succession for a time long enough to exclude any reasonable apprehension of adverse claims, is the only acceptable proof of title in this country.

Defects of title.

So far we have assumed that the possessor starts from what the Romans called a "just cause" of possession: he has purchased from some one who was apparently entitled, or has entered, after the former holder's death, as the nearest heir known or reasonably supposed to be living, or as the person answering a description by which the next taker of the estate has been pointed out in a settlement or will. In any one of these and such like matters, error, though exceptional, is possible. Some element of due form may have been lacking; a man not heard of for many years may have been alive; an obscure disposition may have been wrongly interpreted. Where innocent cause of error exists, it is easy to allow (not to go into details) that the defect shall

[1] As where particular lands have been bestowed and made inalienable by Parliament as a reward for signal public service.

be curable by lapse of time, and that in the meanwhile the possessory title shall be respected by the world at large as if it were perfect. Hugh, a mere stranger, shall not disturb Giles or Giles's heirs and assigns with impunity merely because Peter may have had better right than Giles.

Wrongful possession as origin of rights.

Now let us take the harder case of a possession begun by wrong. With or without a more or less plausible claim of right Peter has turned out John, disseised him as our fathers said, whereas John's title is really the better. Thus Peter starts without any legal merits in his own person, whether he is or not morally excusable. John will of course have his remedy, subject to whatever rules of law require parties to assert their rights within due time. Peter, having gained actual possession, must be protected against mere extraneous violence. That is required, as we have already noted, for the preservation of peace and order. If Peter has done wrong in taking possession, redress is for the true owner to seek, punishment (if any) for the State to inflict. But is a person who comes into Peter's place as heir or purchaser, or the successors of any such person, to be no better off? We have allowed that the apparently rightful possessor is to be treated as owner for purposes of disposition as well as use. Now this principle is admitted partly for his own benefit and protection, but also for the benefit and protection of those who may deal with him as owner on the strength of his apparently rightful title. Considering then the position of a dispossessor, we have to bear in mind that the wrongfulness of his possession is by no means always or necessarily apparent to those who may come after him by purchase or otherwise. They may be and often will be no less deserving than the successors of an apparent owner whose possession began with just cause. Hence it is reasonable to protect them in the same manner as against every one who can show no better right. In so doing the law must take its chance of protecting some persons who are undeserving. But the deserving ones, those who deal in good faith with persons reasonably appearing to be entitled, are the majority, and it is better to favour some unjust than to vex many just occupiers. Thus there is nothing anomalous in accepting possession, without regard to its actual origin, as founding a right which, though subject to whatever better rights may exist, is invested as against the world at large with all the incidents of ownership except the power of using any remedy that, like the Roman Vindication, is appropriated to the full right of ownership. The possessor is in a relative sense an owner; possession, in our English phrase, is a root of title. *Beati possidentes* is a true maxim of law, not a mere empirical expression of the natural advantages arising from actual occupation.

Historical priority of possession to ownership.

The foregoing explanation is of course analytical and taken from a modern point of view. Historically the main outline of the process is much simpler, though the details are extremely complex. The notion of possessing is really both much easier and much earlier than that of owning. Archaic habits of thought find the utmost difficulty in conceiving ownership as severed from possession, or a transfer of anything as being effectual without something like a visible transfer of control, a physical delivery or induction. So far as there is any conception of ownership, it is realised only through possession. The Roman law of *dominium* is essentially modern law. Nay, more, the history of our own system shows us a stage of legal thinking in which the rights of an owner out of possession can be dealt with only by ascribing to him a sort of fictitious possession. English law cannot deny that an occupying farmer is possessed of the farmyard as well as of the pigs, ducks, and geese therein, but it asserts that the landlord is seised of the freehold; and seisin, as even our later books of authority will tell us, was originally nothing but possession.[1] In the case of feudal tenures, where a freeholder owes rent and services to an overlord, the lord is said to be seised of the rent by actual receipt of any part of it; and refusal or failure to pay such rent when duly demanded was a disseisin, entitling the lord to bring the same form of action—an "assize of novel disseisin"—as a freeholder who had been physically turned out of possession.[2] Where there was not and could not be actual possession, medieval lawyers endeavoured to find something as like it as possible. They had at last to face the need of doing without, but the effort was a severe one. Rights which "lie in grant" as distinct from "livery," that is, which can be transferred by written grant only—the grant neither requiring nor admitting a visible handing over or induction—have always been regarded in the Common Law as comparatively weak and precarious. Only within half a century has English legislation authorised the transfer of immovable property in possession without either a real or a fictitious "livery." We shook off the medieval bond of materialism as late as 1845, when Parliament had the courage to declare that corporeal hereditaments

[1] Co. Litt. 17 *a*. [2] *Ibid.* § 233.

should "lie in grant as well as in livery," so as to enable the immediate freehold to be dealt with by simple deed.[1]

Prescription and limitation of actions.

Possession, we have just seen, may have all or most of the advantages of ownership against every one but the true owner, in other words it may confer a relatively good title. But, moreover, it may be enabled by lapse of time to become an absolute title. Possession may ripen into ownership; and this result may be produced either positively by the law declaring that the possessor is fully entitled after a certain time, or negatively by depriving adverse claimants of their remedies if during a certain time they omit to exercise them. The former operation of lapse of time is properly called Prescription, sometimes "positive prescription"; the latter, sometimes called "negative prescription," is familiar in English law as the limitation of actions, and, as a general principle of remedial justice, is not confined to claims for the recovery of land or other property. As regards the acquisition of property, the transformation of possession into ownership (or at all events an indisputable right to possess) is obviously most necessary and important in a system where continuous possession with an apparently

[1] 8 & 9 Vict. c. 106.

rightful title is the principal or only proof of ownership. In a system where ownership is capable of direct proof and official confirmation, as by a registry of titles to land, the importance of possession and prescription tends to diminish, and might even conceivably become a vanishing quantity.[1]

Universality of the problems.

Further historical and comparative details would be out of place here. Perhaps we have been too much tempted in that direction already. But it may be worth remarking in general terms that the relations of possession and ownership in Roman and English law, the difficulties arising out of them, and the devices resorted to for obviating or circumventing those difficulties, offer an amount of resemblance even in detail which is much more striking than the superficial and technical differences. We cannot doubt that these resemblances depend on the nature of the problems to be solved and not on any accidental connection. One system of law may have imitated another in particular doctrines and institutions, but imitation cannot find place in processes extending over two or three centuries, and whose fundamental analogies are externally disguised in almost every possible way.

[1] Maine, *Early Law and Custom*, 352-358; Land Transfer Act, 1875, § 21, and see Sir H. Elphinstone thereon in *Law Quart. Rev.* xi. 357, 362.

Analogies of ownership in servitudes.

How far can the notions of ownership and possession apply to those partial rights over another man's belongings (I purposely use a vague and inartificial word) which are an increment of ownership on the active and a subtraction from it on the passive side? Andrew, as owner of Whiteacre, has a right of way over Peter's estate of Blackacre. This is what Roman law calls a servitude; Whiteacre is the "dominant" and Blackacre the "servient" tenement. English law calls it an easement: in modern times we have borrowed the terms "dominant" and "servient" from Roman or Romanised authorities, and use them freely. Peter and his heirs are bound to let Andrew and his heirs pass and repass by that way. So far Peter's ownership is less; not only because Andrew and his successors in title have the right to use Peter's land for a limited purpose, but because Peter and his successors cannot close or divert the way without their consent. Just so far, on the other hand, the range of Andrew's ownership is increased. Is it correct to call him owner of the easement? He is owner of Whiteacre with the advantage of the easement; that, however, is not quite the same thing; and we must find a closer test. If he could deal with the right of way as a separate thing, set it going by itself as it were, so that some day John, who has nothing to do with Whiteacre, could claim the right of way, and William, or whoever might hold Whiteacre, could not, that would be a distinct ownership indeed. But this is just what neither English nor Roman law will allow to be done. As Lord Cairns said, "There can be no easement properly so called unless there be both a servient and a dominant tenement. . . . There can be no such thing according to our law, or according to the civil law, as what I may term an easement in gross."[1] Andrew can transfer a right of way across Blackacre only by transferring his ownership of Whiteacre; and if John has, as he may have, a personal right, unconnected with ownership of any other land, to use the same way, John cannot transfer that right at all.

No separate possessory rights in servitudes.

Easements and other limited rights over the property of others appear to be as incapable of separate and independent possession as of separate and independent ownership; and this, as to many of them, for the additional reason that the use and enjoyment of them are not exclusive.

A man who has a right of way for walking or

[1] *Rangeley* v. *Midland R. Co.* (1868), L.R. 3 Ch. 306, 311.

driving has neither the power nor the intention to prevent other people from walking or driving the same way. Such persons as may do so without right or leave are trespassers not against him but against the owner of the soil. A person who actually obstructs the use of the way may commit wrongs against both the owner of the soil and the person or persons having a right of way, but not the same wrong. It must be remembered, however, that an exclusive right of occupation, though temporary and for a limited purpose, will confer possession while it lasts.[1] And rights of enjoyment which are exclusive though partial are allowed the benefit of possessory remedies in the Common Law,[2] and in that sense may be said to be capable of quasi-possession, and to be founded on a control of the thing enjoyed, which, though partial and intermittent, is real and exclusive so far as it goes. Lapse of time is available for the acquisition of easements by showing continuous enjoyment of the advantage in question, whatever it may be, as incident to the possession of the dominant tenement, not as being or manifesting a distinct posses-

[1] *Crosby* v. *Wadsworth* (1805), 6 East 602, 8 R.R. 566, and see the Preface to that volume.

[2] Authorities cited in Pollock and Wright on *Possession*, pp. 35-6.

sion. This follows from the principles just stated. Whether a *de facto* enjoyment of an apparent easement really goes along with the title or apparent title to a certain tenement can be known, in the absence of documentary proof, only by the occupation of the tenement being coupled with the enjoyment of the way over another tenement, or whatever other advantage it may be, for such time as the law deems sufficient: of which time, again, the length has to be fixed by a positive rule. It is not necessarily the same length of time that would suffice to make out a title by possession to the alleged dominant tenement itself. General policy would seem to require stricter conditions of prescription in the case of servitudes. For the tenements themselves must (in our law at any rate) belong to somebody; but it is not necessary that there should be any servitude at all between them. The claimant of a servitude is claiming to enlarge his own powers in an exceptional though a recognised manner, and to cut short those of his neighbour. Hence the acquisition of easements by lapse of time may well be purposely made rather difficult. In the law of Scotland, indeed, a definite origin has to be shown in every case, and acquisition by mere lapse of time is not allowed at all.[1] Where a time is allowed and fixed by law as capable of having that effect, it seems on principle that before the expiration of that time there is no right of any sort, and that it would be fallacious to suggest that there can be a quasi-possessory interest deemed worthy of protection against a mere stranger, though not as against the alleged servient tenement itself.[2] It may be added that a theoretical right to assert such an interest could seldom if ever have any useful operation for the claimant. For the third person interfering with the enjoyment of an inchoate easement could always take the line of asserting that he had acted in the interest and by the authority of the owner against whom the easement was in process of being acquired. And it would be that owner's interest to ratify the act, since the acquisition of an adverse right would thus be interrupted, and the interruption put on record, in the most effectual manner, and with the least amount of trouble to himself.

Negative servitudes or easements.

It would lead us too far if we were to approach the various questions of principle raised by those

[1] The fiction of a lost grant in the Common Law may be said to represent a nominal saving of the same principle; the apparent compromise being, however, a virtual abandonment. But this is too technical and difficult a matter to be dwelt on here.

[2] This is almost certainly so in our law. See Holmes, *The Common Law*, p. 241.

adjuncts or outworks of immovable property which consist merely in a right to restrain a neighbour from doing something on his own land. Excavating the soil so as to let down a building on the adjacent estate is one example of such acts. Rights to be free from disturbance due to a neighbour's acts done on his own land, and not otherwise unlawful, may be considered in a particular system of law either as "natural rights" annexed to ownership and not needing to be established by any special proof, or as "negative easements" for which some definite origin other than the character and contiguity of the two tenements must be shown. In either case enjoyment of such rights can offer at most a partial and imperfect analogy to possession. For the legal idea of possession and its consequences is founded on a situation not only of use and enjoyment but of effective control. In these cases, however, the person who profits by his neighbour's forbearance to let down the adjacent ground, to erect buildings which block his lights, and so forth, obviously has no natural control in the matter at all: for he can exercise control only within his own boundaries. His power is just whatever power the law may give him of claiming redress by legal process in the event of disturbance. Again the generality or impersonality of true possession is wanting, for there is nothing which is enjoyed and nothing which can be protected as against the world at large. The only real subject of possession is the tenement to which advantages of this kind may be incident.

Monopolies

One step further brings us to monopolies and franchises which resemble "natural rights" or "negative easements" in the characters just mentioned, or some of them, but are distinct incorporeal things not annexed to any corporeal thing. As we have already pointed out,[1] such rights are capable of having a perfectly definite value and being dealt with as objects of commerce. An exclusive right to ferry passengers across a river at a particular place may be taken as an ancient example of the class. Copyright in a book, performing right in a play, the right to a trade-mark, are familiar in modern business and litigation. Here there is something more like possession than in the case of negative easements; for there are the will and the legal power to exclude the world at large from interference or competition with the exclusive privilege, whatever it may be. But still the legal power is not modelled on any

[1] See p. 131 above.

natural power. Apart from the right to set the law in motion and procure the application of coercive legal process, the author or publisher of a book has no control in fact over the multiplication of copies by unlicensed persons; rather publication involves, as matter of fact, the abandonment of any previously existing control. Still less can it be said that the printer of a pirated edition has usurped or entered upon the author's rights. He has merely committed a wrongful act; he has not acquired anything analogous to the "estate by wrong" of an intruder on land. On the whole it seems that the analogies of possession cannot be safely or profitably applied to rights of this kind.[1]

Extension of ownership to incorporeal franchises.

There is no reason, however, why such rights should not have incidents modelled on those which attach to ownership in the case of corporeal things. Without such incidents, in fact, they would be of comparatively little value. Rights, however profitable, which cannot be transferred by sale are a cumbrous investment, even for a man's own lifetime; rights which will not pass by succession

[1] Illegitimate extensions of the idea of possession were common in the continental speculation of the Middle Ages, and not unknown in England. See Co. Litt. 113 *b*; Dernburg, Pandekten, i. § 191.

or bequest are useless as a provision for a man's family. We find, in fact, that these incorporeal rights and advantages, patents, trade-marks, copyrights, and the like, are transferable and alienable, as nearly as may be, after the manner of corporeal things of value. Still there is only an approximation to ownership, for there is not any general power of use or enjoyment, only the receipt of profits increased by the particular advantage of competition being excluded. A patentee has not any right to do what he could not have done without a patent, but the right to prevent other people from competing with him in the manufacture and sale of his invention. The language about "property in ideas" used by some modern writers appears to be founded on a confusion of essentially different conceptions. A monopoly in the reproduction of particular forms of literary or artistic representation, or the performance or the manufacture and sale of a new invention, of a musical or dramatic work, is that which it has been made by law, or possibly, in some cases, by usage outside law,[1] and it is not anything else. Whether the law shall confer such monopolies on authors and inventors, to what extent in point

[1] See p. 125 above.

of duration and otherwise, and subject to what conditions, is a question of expediency on which little, if any, light seems to be thrown by the institution of ownership in corporeal things, notwithstanding that the analogy has been dwelt upon as a valid one by some considerable authorities.[1]

Right to privacy distinguished.

The right of preventing the publication of unpublished materials is of a different kind; in English authorities it is commonly derived, as regards manuscripts, original drawings, and the like, from an owner's general right of restraining the world at large from any kind of unauthorised intermeddling with his property. Yet this principle is hardly sufficient for all cases. There is no doubt that the receiver or holder of a private letter may not publish it without the writer's consent, although there is also no doubt that the paper may be his property for all other purposes; he cannot be required, for example, as between

[1] Much discussion of the principles involved in the question of "copyright at common law" may be found in the great case of *Jefferys* v. *Boosey* (1854), 4 H.L.C. 815, where, however, it is unavoidably mixed up with points of detail arising on the facts. The arguments for and against the existence of such a right are most distinctly put in the opinions of Erle, J., Maule, J., and Coleridge, J. (*pro*); and Pollock, C.B., Lord Brougham, and Lord St. Leonards (*contra*). The negative conclusion is now generally accepted by lawyers. Mr. Herbert Spencer, whose philosophy of political and legal institutions really belongs to the eighteenth century, has consistently maintained the older view.

himself and the writer, to preserve it. We have then to say that a letter is given by the writer to the receiver under an implied condition that it is not to be published without the writer's consent. But it is hard to see, on any accepted legal principles, how such a condition can be enforced against any third person into whose hands the letter may come. There is much to be said for the suggestion recently made in America, and supported with great ability and ingenuity by its authors, that every citizen is entitled to a certain measure of privacy in his own affairs, as a branch of the general right to personal immunity; that this right, as applied to the communication of one's thoughts or sentiments to the public, is not limited to cases where the expression of them happens to be embodied in some tangible record such as a manuscript or drawing; and that it is independent of the right of property in any such tangible object.[1] Of course there is no objection to the right of property, where it does happen to be available, being used in aid of the more general and personal right; and as this is the safer course when it is possible, a long time may yet

[1] "The Right to Privacy," by Samuel D. Warren and Louis D. Brandeis, *Harv. Law Rev.* iv. 193.

elapse before the fundamental question is decided either by authority or by a consensus of reasoned opinion.

Incorporea property consisting in obligations.

There are yet other incorporeal things to which the analogy of ownership is largely applied. In the language of common life and business we have no difficulty and no sense of incongruity in saying that a man owns or possesses money in the funds, railway shares or debentures, or other investments which really consist in a claim to interest or to a share of profits in proportion to the capital sum invested. Nowadays it is not usual, and may seem hardly natural, to call a merchant the owner of the debts growing due to him in the course of his business; there is no doubt, however, that such debts count as a part of his property; they are assets; they may well form a considerable part of all he is worth. And in the case of many securities and investments there is a true possession and ownership of the documents by which the right of the holder is proved. What is more, in some cases, namely, those of negotiable instruments, ownership or even possession of a material document is the only normal proof of right to the payment secured or promised by its terms. Thus the resemblance to ownership of corporeal goods is very strong at first sight. But, before we can judge how far this resemblance holds, we must consider more closely the nature of the rights arising out of claims of one definite person against another, or, in the accustomed term of the Roman lawyers, obligations. We have already touched in a general way on the distinction between impersonal and personal duties. It is now time to attend to its principal consequences.

CHAPTER VIII

CLAIMS OF PERSONS ON PERSONS: RELATION OF OBLIGATIONS TO PROPERTY

Personal duties definite or indefinite.

In the last chapter we spoke of rights available against the world at large. Mutual duties and rights between certain persons and groups of persons, not shared by the world at large, likewise exist by law and custom in all settled communities. They may be seen at once to fall into two classes, namely, those which are definite and those which are indefinite. The relations of husband and wife and parent and child give rise to duties and claims which are strictly personal. But these are not separate and independent duties. They are incident to the continuous relation of the parties; they cannot be exhausted by any enumeration of particulars; and they cannot be brought to an end except by the expiration or determination of the personal relation to which they are incident. The advantages and benefits arising from them are not recognised by law, not by modern law at any rate, as a possible subject-matter of sale, barter, or traffic of any kind, or of adequate pecuniary estimation.[1] Hence those advantages and benefits, however important to individuals and to society, are not things in the legal sense. Besides all this the family relations belong, to a large extent, to the sphere of moral as distinct from that of legal justice and right. Courts of law can deal only with the grosser infractions and shortcomings that occur in family affairs. It is true that the Church of Rome has attempted, and in the Middle Ages did habitually accomplish, a great extension of formal doctrine and jurisdiction as regards marriage and sexual morality generally. The results are matter of history, and appear, to the English lay mind at any rate, to stand as warning rather than as example.

Family relations and the duties arising from them present, in short, analogies to the rights of

[1] The remedies allowed by the Common Law for violation of marital or parental rights are directed only to certain incidents of the right, not the right as a whole.

property and possession on the one hand, and to rights created by agreement of parties on the other; but they are also marked by essential differences which place them apart, and make it dangerous to trust any such analogies for the purpose of deducing consequences.

The other great class of duties and rights taking effect between ascertained persons are those which have regard to some definite performance or observance to be rendered by one party to another. When we say that the performance or observance is definite, we mean that it is definite enough for the law to pronounce, in case of dispute, whether it is duly fulfilled or not, and also to set a pecuniary value upon it. These distinctions have already been pointed out in considering the current divisions of legal rules.[1]

Obligations merely personal in early law.

At first sight it would seem that a claim with a corresponding duty, subsisting between two definite persons, concerns those two persons only, and the rights constituting or flowing from such a claim cannot have any resemblance to the rights of an owner. This is in fact the view taken in all or almost all early systems of law. Roman law,

[1] Ch. iv. p. 79 above.

though modified in practice in the later classical period, never ceased on principles to treat obligations as having an essentially personal character. The benefit of what is due to one by agreement cannot be made over to a third person in any of the ways in which corporeal things, or limited rights over them, are conveyed.[1] For the debtor, it is said, cannot become bound to a new creditor without his own consent, that is, without a new agreement or "novation." If I want to assign my rights, I must get my debtor and the new creditor to make a fresh contract. Perhaps this view was not always a merely technical or logical one. For most archaic laws, including those of Rome, gave a creditor enormous powers of self-redress, even to imprisoning and practically enslaving the debtor in default of payment.[2] Under such a system the personal character and temper of the creditor might obviously be no less important to the debtor than the debtor's honesty or means of payment to the creditor. Apart from this reason, however, the

[1] Obligationes quoquo modo contractae nihil eorum recipiunt: nam quod mihi ab aliquo debetur, id si velim tibi deberi, nullo eorum modo quibus res corporales ad alium transferuntur id efficere possum.—Gai. ii. 38.

[2] Muirhead, *Hist. Intr. to the Private Law of Rome*, 155, and references there given for early Germanic law. Similar powers are found in Asiatic customs.

strictly personal view of obligations created by agreement is appropriate, in the unqualified form of the classical Roman doctrine, only to a world where there is, we need not even say no credit or no money, but no common measure of values. In modern law we have to distinguish for this purpose between different kinds of contracts, namely, those which are for special performances or services, those which are for the transfer of property, and those which are for the payment of money; and, within this last class, those which are only for the settlement of private affairs and those which are intended to create exchangeable value.

Personal contracts in modern law.

Some agreements are really such that they can be performed only between the original parties, inasmuch as they involve the exercise of personal skill in a specially designated manner, or mutual relations of personal confidence, or both. Examples of this are undertakings to execute a work of literature or art, and agreements to enter into active partnership in a business requiring special knowledge or training. Obviously the rights arising out of such transactions are neither proper nor practicable objects of exchange. Not proper, because the person who is bound is generally more or less influenced by personal considerations. It is by no means to be assumed that a painter who has undertaken to paint a picture, say for the town-hall of his native city, would have chosen to paint it for a stranger on the same terms, or at all. Not practicable, because the right to a special and personal performance is valuable only to a limited class of persons or to one person, even when that kind of performance is so far in general request as to have a market of its own and an ascertainable market value. There is no difficulty in knowing approximately for what price a good tailor will make a suit of clothes; but when a man has been measured for a suit of clothes, the right to have that particular suit is not worth the tailor's price, or anything like it, to any one but himself. Again the price of a railway ticket (that is, of the railway company's undertaking to carry one, with due care, and on other express and implied terms of reciprocal duty, between the specified stations) is as fixed as any price can be; but a railway ticket from Oxford to Plymouth is in fact[1] worthless to a man at Oxford who does not want to go to Plymouth.

[1] As things are: but conditions may well be conceived (*e.g.* a system of State or municipal railways with uniform "zone" fares, and tickets available over a considerable time for any one of several lines) under which railway tickets might become an auxiliary currency, as postage stamps now are to a certain extent.

Or, to go back to more personal relations, the services of a qualified conveyancing clerk are worth much in a solicitor's office, but would be worth nothing in an engineer's. In all these cases, therefore, the person entitled to the performance or service, whatever it may be, cannot be said to be in a position like an owner's. The performance will give him some advantage or profit, something that he wants and has a value for, or he would not have bargained for it; perhaps it will make him the owner of a thing not only valuable to himself in the way of personal use or pleasure, but having a considerable value in exchange, as in the case of a picture to be painted. But in the meantime he has nothing under his own control, and, except by some unusual accident, nothing that he can count on being able to dispose of.

Contracts for sale: their connection with ownership.

Next let us consider those agreements which are directed to a change of ownership as their main object: that is, agreements for sale and purchase. Here we have a connection with owners' rights, and a very close one. A buyer of a specific thing who has paid, or is ready and willing to pay, or to whom credit has been given by the seller, may call at any moment for the thing he has bought. Or he may direct the seller to deal with it on his behalf, to make it over to some third person for example, provided that the seller is not put to any cost or risk beyond what was undertaken by the original agreement. In short the buyer has every lawful disposing power, though he may not be able to prevent the seller from playing false before possession of the thing has been actually transferred. The seller on the other hand has no longer any rightful active interest in the thing; he holds it only for the buyer. So the step from enforcing concluded agreements to transfer property to regarding the transfer itself as complete by virtue of the agreement is an easy and short one, and has been made in more than one system of law. In modern France a contract for the sale of corporeal things, whether movable or immovable, passes the property forthwith as between the parties. This is also the rule of the Common Law (though not of very ancient date) as regards goods. With regard to land the king's judges at Westminster, true to Germanic principles and in conformity (probably unconscious) with Roman maxims, held otherwise, but the more subtle and expansive justice of the Chancellors made its honour and profit of their adherence to the old ways. The king's equity administered by his Chancellor, which became in course of time the settled law of the Court of Chancery, was ready to compel the seller to make good his agreement and convey the land to the ready and willing buyer. But it did more; it treated the buyer in the meantime as owner for all substantial purposes. It looked on him as having an "equitable estate" in the land, not a mere personal claim. The buyer has an interest which he can resell,[1] settle on his family in his lifetime, or dispose of by will. He has everything except the complete security of an owner as against the world at large: the Court of Chancery could not give him the "legal estate" which only a real delivery of legal possession, or something equivalent, can take from one holder and confer on another. The barrier that stands between an "equitable owner" and full ownership is the risk of being displaced by a "purchaser for value without notice," to whom the property is sold or made a security by the fraud or other fault of the legal and apparent owner, but without any fault or neglect of the purchaser's.[2] Subject to that risk, the man who

[1] See *Wood* v. *Griffith* (1818). 1 Sw. 43, 18 R.R. 18.

[2] Details of our doctrine on these matters, a subtle doctrine, but a just and salutary one in the main, would be out of place here. *Pilcher* v. *Rawlins* (1872), L.R. 7 Ch. 259, contains the leading authoritative exposition of the principles.

has an effectual right by contract to be made the owner of real estate in countries under the Common Law has the rights and advantages of property without waiting for the actual transfer. Accordingly the benefit of an obligation whose object is the transfer of property not only has a definite value and is property in the larger sense, but cannot have the name of property refused to it even in the stricter sense.

Contracts for payment.

Let us now proceed to contracts whose object is to make a man owner not of goods or land having an ascertainable value, but of the medium and measure of exchangeable values itself: in other words, contracts for the payment of money. The right to call for a certain sum of money, supposing that payment can be counted on, is as useful and valuable, except for merely "petty cash" transactions, as the money itself. In many ways and on many occasions, indeed, it is even more useful. And, like the money itself, it must be taken, for all purposes capable of reduction to general statement or rule, and therefore for legal purposes amongst others, to have the same value for every one. Therefore it is by its nature an exchangeable commodity. Men of business will treat it as such, and the law of modern commercial States must recognise it as such, even at the cost of doing apparent violence to principles derived from a different kind of experience. The Common Law, before the middle of the eighteenth century, was slow to bring itself into line with the usage of mankind; but, under the impulse given in a critical period by Lord Mansfield's genius, the expansion, when it came, was swift and full.[1] Credit has become currency in law as well as in fact.

Special forms of transferable contract.

We have said that payment of the debt must be assumed as practically certain; or, to speak more exactly, the risk of default must at most be small enough to be outweighed by the convenience of doing business between distant places without the risk and cost of constantly transmitting coined metal or bullion. Now this risk and cost, which are considerable even at the present day, were so great in the Middle Ages that a very moderate standard of credit might well suffice to make the use of credit preferable. But there must be some means of keeping credit at a fairly uniform working level by excluding disputes in matter of fact. No man will take a book debt due to a tradesman as

[1] The French doctrine of negotiable instruments, having been prematurely codified, is still much less advanced from a mercantile point of view than the English or Anglo-American. See Chalmers on *Bills of Exchange*, Introduction, at pp. liv. lv., 4th ed. 1891.

equivalent to the nominal amount of the bill. Apart from the trouble of collection and the possible doubt whether the customer will pay, there may be undisclosed grounds of difficulty. If it be a tailor's bill, the customer may object that the clothes do not fit; if a bookseller's, there may be a claim for abatement on the score of imperfect or wrongly described copies; and the like, with endless variety of particulars, in other cases. Hence a debt which is to be the foundation of truly and freely exchangeable value must be unconditionally acknowledged, and evidenced in an understood form which marks it off beyond mistake from debts liable to extraneous causes of dispute. Again there must be clear and ready means of letting the debtor know whom he is to pay. This is needful in the interest of all parties. For it is "a rule of general jurisprudence," as was said by a great master of law, "that if a person enters into a contract, and, without notice of any assignment, fulfils it to the person with whom he made the contract, he is discharged from his obligation."[1] Further, the obligation must be reinforced by the custom and public opinion of the class of persons most concerned, namely, merchants. About the

[1] Willes, J., in *De Nicholls* v. *Saunders*, L.R. 5 C.P. at p. 594.

second quarter of the fourteenth century the ingenuity of Mediterranean traders provided for all these requirements by establishing the main features of bills of exchange, out of which the whole system of modern credit has grown.[1] Risk of the parties originally or ultimately liable being insolvent can, of course, not be wholly eliminated, though measures of precaution and mitigation are possible. Risks of fraud and forgery likewise exist, but these differ only in degree from the risk of taking bad money when one is dealing with hard cash.

Negotiable instruments and paper currency.

But it is not enough to give the ordinary incidents of property to commercial obligations if they are to be effective instruments of commerce and adjusters of mutual credits. A currency must have more than the common capacity of passing by transfer. It must pass without discussion of the holder's ownership, so long as it is genuine. The very purpose of current coin is not merely to measure values, but to free the receiver of a payment from having to trace back the payer's right to what he hands over. Such is the real difference between sale and barter: and so needful to current money is this quality of dispensing with proof of title,

[1] See examples and references collected by Mr. E. Jenks, "Early History of Negotiable Instruments," *Law Quart. Rev.* x. 73 *sqq.*

or, as our ancestors would have said, neither requiring nor admitting warranty, that it is assumed in every system of law as being too elementary to call for definition or authority. Credit has been put on an equal footing with metallic currency in this respect by making bills of exchange and other like documents not only transferable but negotiable. Paper money and other instruments payable to bearer are transferable not like ordinary goods, but like the coin which they potentially[1] represent, and the right to receive what is expressed to be due passes with the document and is inseparable from it. Thus we have a large and most important class of incorporeal things, and moreover things consisting in obligation, which are not only alienable, but more fully and freely alienable than almost every kind of corporeal things, and so connected with particular corporeal things—namely, the negotiable documents themselves—that possession of such a thing in good faith and for value conclusively determines the right. Although this does not make it correct to say that the holder of a bill of

[1] Potentially because negotiable paper can actually represent nothing but credit, however good the credit may be. The promise of the Bank of England to pay £5 is as good as £5 in gold, but still a promise. And this remains true even when we are bound by law to accept that promise as "legal tender."

exchange has a thing in possession (for the actual piece of paper, being valuable only for the sake of the incorporeal right which it represents, does not count as a corporeal thing of value),[1] the fact of rights arising from contract being thus intimately associated with possession and physical delivery shows how far modern developments of business have taken us from the old personal and inalienable character of obligations.

Shares and other modern forms of investment.

Another kind of alienable obligations are those which constitute the great bulk of permanent investments. Government and other securities, joint-stock shares, and the like, are nothing else (apart from any eventual liability to which they may expose the holders in some cases) than the right to receive a fixed rate of interest or annuity, or a dividend or share of profits not fixed, but often capable of approximate estimation beforehand. Such rights are as much property as the capital invested; whether they are a good equivalent for

[1] On the other hand the offence of theft was defined at a relatively early stage in the history of English law, and, as defined, involved a wrongful change of possession in a corporeal thing of value. The result of different parts of the law remaining in such different states of development was that, until a remedy was provided by legislation, no taking of documents whose sole value was in "their evidentiary character" could be theft: an absurd but not a capricious result.—See Pollock and Wright on *Possession*, 233-5.

it is a question of fact with which legal principle has nothing to do. In fact we commonly regard a holder of stock or shares as still having the capital, and think of the interest or dividends as being the fruits of capital in the same way that rent and agricultural profits are the fruits of land. And this is substantially true for economic purposes, but legally the capital, as the investor's capital, does not exist: it has become the firm's or company's capital.[1] In the same way every one who keeps a banking account will talk of his money at the bank, though he has really parted with whatever has been paid in, and his balance is simply a balance of unsecured debt from the banker. More generally, it is said with truth that "the lender of money thinks the money lent still belongs to him, and that the borrower has acquired only the right to use it temporarily";[2] and this conception was the predominant one in early law and procedure, as our old English forms of action abundantly witness. An overdue debt was treated as a thing which the

[1] The case of stock in the public funds is even stronger; there the fundholder is entitled, in law and in fact, only to certain annual payments. There is no right to repayment of the principal sum at any assignable time or under any assignable conditions: "the principal is a purely fictitious amount; it is merely a cipher by which the interest is computed."—C. Sweet in *L.Q.R.* x. 303.

[2] Langdell, *Summary of Contracts*, § 99.

borrower unjustly withheld from the lender, as he might have kept a borrowed horse or "held over" in the occupation of a piece of land. Possession of land and payment of money were claimed in precisely similar forms of words. Here popular archaism reinforces the modern business way of treating affairs. With the great majority of investors in either the public funds or the debentures or shares of a company the difficulty would be, not to persuade them that their interests are really property, but to make them understand how there can be anything about so simple a fact that needs explanation. Such interests are alienable and are largely bought and sold every day; they are often the staple of men's estates, and are made the provision of families. In some cases permanent securities[1] are not only alienable but negotiable; such cases are exceptional in English usage, but by no means uncommon in America.

Accordingly rights to performance or payment

[1] The difference between lending on the security of an undertaking (as on debentures) and adventuring one's money in the undertaking (as in ordinary shares) is of minor importance for our general purpose. Here we must say "securities": ordinary shares or stock cannot be negotiable for want of a definite and unconditional promise to pay. If not fully paid up, they involve a contingent liability which would make another fatal obstacle to their being negotiable as distinct from transferable.

Rights created by contract may be property: distinction as to other obligations.

created by agreement are things in contemplation of law, so far as they have a value for the person entitled, which courts of justice will define or recognise as defined by the parties. And, beyond this, definite rights arising from agreement not only are things, but can be made exchangeable things, property in the fullest sense, if such is the intention of the parties, and if that intention is recognised by rules of law as deserving encouragement on grounds of general convenience. Obligations independent of the consent of parties remain to be considered under the same aspect. The right in these cases may be a right either to specific restitution in some form, or, as it is much more commonly, to compensation in money. Private rights to receive fixed sums of money by way of compensation or forfeiture are also possible, but in modern law not very frequent.[1] In any of these alternatives the plaintiff's right is at least capable of being assessed in terms of money; he will get money or money's worth. He is better off, by an assignable amount, than if his right were not recognised by law.[2] So far there does not appear any reason for refusing to

[1] In our law stipulations for fixed penalties or "liquidated damages" are constantly treated as only fixing a maximum compensation.

[2] See Dr. Moyle's *Justinian*, 2nd ed. p. 189.

include obligations of this kind in the category of things. If they were further recognised by law, like pecuniary rights created by agreement, as possible objects of exchange and traffic, there could be no hesitation about including them. But they are distinctly not so recognised. It is not thought good for justice, peace, or fair dealing that hostile rights of action should be marketable. This principle is found, I believe, in all civilised laws; it is at the bottom of the rules of the Common Law against "maintenance" and "champerty," rules which at first sight look technical and even capricious, but which were called forth by real dangers and abuses. No doubt it may be hard to draw the line between a genuine sale of property with a title more or less capable of doubt and the sale of a speculative lawsuit. Our ancestors were disposed to draw it by requiring actual possession as a condition of effectually dealing with property, or in the case of incorporeal things the nearest possible equivalent of possession. Whether modern lawyers can accept so trenchant a solution or not, the line still has to be drawn somewhere; and rights and interests that fall on the wrong side of it will not be lawful objects of commerce.

In the case, then, of claims arising from wrong-

Rights arising from wrongful acts are not exchangeable things, *qu.* whether to be called things at all.

ful acts, or from acts or events not necessarily wrongful in themselves but having like effects under particular rules of law, we have to ask whether rights valuable to the person entitled, but not alienable, are to be considered as things. Perhaps this is a question of terms more than of substance. There is no doubt that Roman lawyers, though they would have been shocked at the notion of treating rights to sue for injuries as exchangeable property, did regard them as things of some kind; and they seem to be included in the "things in action" of the medieval Common Law, so far as it has any defined terminology. Modern usage may tend, on the other hand, to treat not only some present intrinsic worth but some worth in exchange, and therefore capacity of exchange, as essential to the notion of a thing. On this view the right to recover damages or obtain restitution, though valuable, is not a thing at all. The contrast between such duties and rights as are created or accepted by the will of the parties, or defined as in accordance with what is deemed to be the will of reasonable parties, and such as are imposed by rules of law without regard to the will of the parties, has already been mentioned, and attention has been called to its increasing importance in modern affairs.

It would attain a further degree of recognition, as it were an added emphasis, if the view now suggested were generally adopted, and, instead of saying with the Romans that certain things have not exchangeable value or are not allowed to be exchanged, we said that whatever has not lawful exchangeable value, be it corporeal or incorporeal, is not a thing in the eye of the law.

PART II

LEGAL AUTHORITIES AND THEIR USE

CHAPTER I

THE EXPRESS FORMS OF LAW

Law can be known only as stated.

LAW, for the practical purposes of lawyers and citizens, means (as in effect we said earlier) the sum of those rules of conduct which courts of justice enforce, the conditions on which they become applicable, and the manner and consequences of their application. This is a matter of fact not in any way dependent on the view that we may take of the political and ethical foundations of government and positive law, still less on the correctness or adequacy of any philosophical definition of law in general by which views of that kind are formulated. The rules of law, like those of every other science and art, have to be brought to our knowledge by means of articulate statements. But in this case the form of such statements is of peculiar importance.

Forms of stating law.

The express forms in which we come to know any system of law may be generally classified thus:

A. Command.

B. Maxim or text.

C. Interpretation.

We take this as a classification of observed facts, and without regard, for the immediate purpose in hand, to the controverted question on which we have already touched,[1] but which belongs really not to jurisprudence but to the philosophy of politics, whether and to what extent positive law can be accounted for as a whole by the express or implied command of the sovereign power in the commonwealth. There can be no doubt that, in point of form, some statements of law are commands and others are not. The former (A) may conveniently be called imperative, the latter (B and C) discursive.

Commands.

Command purports to proceed from and to express the will of some power claiming obedience and expecting to be obeyed.[2]

Maxims.

A legal maxim or text may or may not purport

[1] Part I., ch. i.

[2] These are not the same thing. During a great part of the eighteenth century the Pretender claimed the obedience of Englishmen as his subjects, but experience proved that he could not in fact expect the majority of them to obey him.

to be derived either directly or remotely from the command of a legislator.

Interpretation. Interpretation is the scientific process of applying legal rules in detail. It necessarily assumes the existence and authority[1] of the rules which it explains and applies. It may or may not claim or possess authority of its own.

Written law. "Written law," as the phrase is commonly used, does not mean rules of law expressed in writing, but what we have called *imperative* law, an express precept which not only declares or contains, but in its very words constitutes the law.

Unwritten law. "Unwritten law" includes all *discursive* expressions of law, however carefully they may be reduced to writing, and whatever their professional authority or weight may be. Thus an Act of Parliament, a by-law of a local authority, the articles of an incorporated company, are written laws; a judgment of the Court of Appeal, delivered after consideration, and printed in the current reports, is "unwritten" law. The term, though easily misunderstood, and at first sight paradoxical,

[1] Such assumption may be limited or relative, as when English Protestant judges interpret Roman canon law, *e.g.* in a Maltese marriage case; or it may be for argument's sake only, as when it is sought to show that a proposed rule cannot be law because it leads to absurd consequences.

is not improper. For the words of the judgment, however precise, are still an exposition of the law and not the law itself. Only the principle expounded and applied by the court is law; the words in which it is explained are not binding on any one.

Let us now mark somewhat more closely the special characters of the forms of law we have noted.

Command: actual or legendary.

A. Command, in the way of systematic legislation, has been said to be the form of law which tends to prevail in modern times. Be that as it may, we cannot say that any other form is more ancient. Archaic law, so far as preserved to us, is quite commonly thus expressed. The Ten Commandments and the Twelve Tables, widely separated as they are in place and time, are the most familiar examples. "Hominem mortuum in urbe ne sepelito neve urito" is the precursor in form as in substance (whether the real motive of the prohibition were sanitary or religious) of our latest Public Health Acts.

Not only this, but there is a marked tendency even in relatively modern times to refer existing rules of law and customs, though not preserved in any authentic form of words, to the express institution of some heroic person of a former generation. One of the first signs of revived English feeling after the Norman Conquest was a demand for the restoration of laws of Edward the Confessor which had never been made. In like manner trial by jury had barely taken anything like its modern shape when pious antiquaries began to ascribe it to the ordinance of King Alfred. All the ancient Hindu law-books, and some that are not very ancient, profess to represent the utterance of some inspired sage.

B. Legal maxims and texts are produced, in different ways and in different stages of legal development, by the practical needs of suitors and of lawyers after a distinct legal profession has come into existence.

Maxim: distinguished from command and explanation.

A maxim is a phrase embodying some legal idea of common application in a concise and portable form. It is a symbol or vehicle of the law, so far as it goes; it is not the law itself, still less the whole of the law, even on its own ground. One of the commonest mistakes of beginners and laymen is to take a maxim for an authentic and complete expression of the law, and go about to deduce consequences from its words as if it were a modern Act of Parliament. The mistake was pointed out many centuries ago by Paulus, and not many years ago by Lord Esher.

"Regula est quae rem quae est breviter enarrat. Non ex regula ius sumatur, sed ex iure quod est regula fiat."[1]

"I detest the attempt to fetter the law by maxims. They are almost invariably misleading: they are for the most part so large and general in their language that they always include something which really is not intended to be included in them."[2]

Another common mistake is to cite maxims as if they contained the reason or explanation of the rules embodied by them, whereas they seldom explain anything, and are almost always subject to implied exceptions and limitations. Thus the sentence *Qui facit per alium facit per se* may be useful as a reminder that acts of a servant about his master's business are (within certain limits) imputed to the master so as to make him answerable for them, whether they were in fact authorised by the master or not. But it does not make the rule in any way more intelligible, or throw any light on its origin. *Sic utere tuo ut alienum non*

[1] D. 50, 17, *de reg. iur.* 1.

[2] Lord Esher, M.R., *Yarmouth* v. *France* (1887), 19 Q.B. Div. 653.

laedas is a precept of law in the nature of a maxim; it holds largely but by no means universally, for though a man may not altogether "do what he will with his own," there are many things he may do without being bound to save his neighbours harmless from any loss or inconvenience that may result. What the maxim really tells us is that the law does set some limits, in the interest of the neighbours and mankind at large, to an owner's use of his property for his own purposes, and every owner must keep within those limits at his peril. The maxim does not profess to tell us what they are. In fact we have here two maxims or proverbs which are in verbal conflict, either of them taken alone and literally being far too wide; if we take them together they roughly limit one another.

Growth of authentic texts.

A certain number of legal texts not being the direct utterance of any supreme power or lawgiver are nevertheless regarded as more or less authentic statements of the law. Such texts have, for the most part, been originally nothing but private comment or interpretation; often they have been the work of persons who expressly disclaimed any pretension to speak with authority, as, in our own country, Littleton. In some cases authority has been conferred on them by special acts of the sovereign power; the great example of this is the treatment of the writings of the classical Roman lawyers which have come down to us in the Digest of Justinian. In other cases private writings have been approved and relied on by lawyers and judges until they have acquired an intrinsic value, and their statements are accepted as authentic or at least presumably correct. This has happened with the English law-texts known as "books of authority," of which we shall say more at a later stage.

Interpretation: its necessity.

C. Interpretation is the process of fixing the application of legal principles in concrete cases, whether the principles be laid down in precise and imperative terms by a lawgiver, or implied in a current rule which has to be sought in "unwritten" law. Some such process is required by the multitude and variety of human affairs, and it is not necessarily connected with any imperfection in the law itself. If the lawgiver says "thou shalt do no murder," it has to be settled what killing is murder. If he says "thou shalt not steal," it has to be settled what kinds of taking or appropriation are theft. And although it may at first seem easy to untrained common sense to pronounce that some acts are within the prohibition of the law and others are not, there will and must be cases near the border-line which are not obviously on either one side or the other. This, moreover, remains true in some measure, however carefully and with whatever amount of detail the law be laid down. What is called the rule against perpetuities in our own law—a modern rule of a highly refined system—limits the time during which the full and final destination of interests in property within the rule may be kept in suspense. In the course of the eighteenth century the limit was decided to be "a life or lives in being, and one and twenty years afterwards." These are Blackstone's words.[1] Fully two generations after Blackstone wrote the question arose, and had to be decided, whether these one and twenty years did or did not involve reference to an actual minority of some person. Although the rule had never been so laid down, there were plausible grounds for thinking that such was its meaning, as any one who knows the history of the doctrine, or knows enough law to make himself acquainted with it, may readily satisfy himself. The House of Lords decided that the twenty-one years were an absolute term "in gross" and need not have regard to any minority.[2]

Every question of interpretation may be reduced

[1] *Comm.* ii. 174. [2] *Cadell* v. *Palmer* (1833), 1 Cl. & F. 372.

ultimately to this form: Given a rule of law that conditions generically described as A produce a certain legal liability or other consequence X, does the specific fact or group of facts *n* fall within the genus A?

Inasmuch as no general rule can anticipate all possible questions of this kind, the need of interpretation is not in itself any reproach to the law. Rather law without interpretation is but a skeleton without life, and interpretation makes it a living body.[1]

It may with equal verbal correctness be affirmed in one sense, and denied in another, that interpretation (whether performed by judges or by text-writers) makes new law. The question may be important in a purely philosophical discussion of law, but for any other purpose it is like discussing whether the John Milton who wrote *Samson Agonistes* was really the same John Milton who wrote *Lycidas.*

The *construction* of written documents, whether of public authority or binding as between private persons, is a special branch of interpretation, and a highly important one, but must by no means be supposed to be the whole of it. Individual actions,

[1] Cp. Sohm's *Institutes of Roman Law*, § 8.

or a course of conduct, may be the subject of interpretation no less than words.

Divers methods of interpretation: case-law.

Interpretation may be carried on, and its results preserved for use, in more than one way, and in fact there have been considerable differences of method according to time, place, and the system of law in force. In England, and countries which have derived their law from England, or come under the influence of English judicial habits, the decisions of superior courts of justice, and the reasons given for them, are chiefly relied on for this purpose, and are treated as having eminent and all but exclusive authority. A judgment prepared by an English judge and delivered in an actual case before the court, or even delivered without preparation, is on a quite distinct footing from any opinion which the same judge may express out of court on the same subject, say in a published treatise on that branch of the law. The judicial deliverance is of authority, unless and until it be reversed or overruled by a higher court; that is, other judges will follow it in similar cases when they occur. The extra-judicial opinion, however carefully formed and expressed, is a mere repertory of arguments; lawyers may find them useful, judges may find them convincing and decide accordingly; but the opinion, as an opinion, is not binding on any one.[1] We shall explain more fully in a subsequent chapter the details of English judicial usage as to the following of decided cases. It is eminently a matter of practical usage, established for something like six centuries in England, though we cannot point to any definite time when it was first adopted, and there has been in proportion to its importance but little formal statement or discussion of it. *Case-law* is now the usual term for the law declared and developed by judicial decisions, and embodied in published reports of them.

Roman system of authoritative writings.

Familiar as this system is to all English lawyers and (to a certain extent) men of affairs who are not lawyers, and natural as it may appear, it is by no means the only possible way of producing a body of scientific material for the guidance of lawyers in advising their clients, and judges in deciding the clients' cases when brought into court. There may be a considerable legal literature, and something like what English lawyers call authority, without the actual decisions of courts of justice being regarded as binding in subsequent cases,

[1] "There is one notion often expressed with regard to works written or revised by authors on the bench, which seems to me in part at least erroneous, the notion, I mean, that they possess a quasi-judicial authority."—Preface to "Fry on Specific Performance," cited by Kekewich, J., *Union Bank* v. *Munster* (1887), 37 Ch.D. at p. 54.

or having any influence at all on professional opinion. Such was the state of Roman law in the republican period; and under the Empire it was probably the combination of judicial with legislative functions in the Emperor's person that caused his judicial deliverances to be accepted as authentic declarations of the law. The ordinary judges were not professional lawyers, nor (in the earlier period) permanent officers of the State; therefore their decisions were of no particular weight, and the scientific development of law was carried on not in court, but (as we should say) in chambers, by the leading lawyers, and in the books and commentaries, perhaps originally meant only for private use, which they produced. The foundation of the Corpus Juris was laid not in the decisions of courts but in the opinions and discussions of advocates. As this book is not an introduction to Roman law, we purposely say nothing of the steps by which the published opinions of the principal Roman jurists acquired a character of positive authority, and ultimately, so far as selected and preserved by Justinian, became "written law."[1]

The pure Roman system, as we may call it,

[1] See Sohm, *Institutes of Roman Law*, §§ 15, 16.

of interpretation founded on extrajudicial opinion has not prevailed to any great extent in modern times. In most continental countries the decisions of the courts are referred to and used in argument or discussion, though the courts are distinctly not bound to follow previous decisions. Exactly speaking, decisions have neither more nor less authority in France, Germany, or Italy at the present day than the opinions of learned persons expressed in any other form. In France, accordingly, it is not uncommon to cite the judgment of a foreign tribunal administering what is really the same law; for example, the construction put on an article of the Code Napoléon by a Belgian court: and there would be no formal objection to citing for the same purpose a judgment of our own Judicial Committee on appeal from Mauritius or the Province of Quebec. In practice, however, it is found that wherever decided cases are made accessible by regular reporting their influence tends to gain on other forms of "scientific law," and jurisprudence to assume a more distinctly national character.

Political and administrative changes which strengthen the courts, increase the proportion of enacted to customary law, and magnify the importance of particular judicial centres, have the like effect. This has been notably the case in Germany during the last generation. It is quite possible that before the end of the century modern German law may practically consist of codes or statutes and case-law.

Effects of royal authority in England

As matter of history, there is no reason to doubt that our own peculiar and definite system of case-law is due to the early assertion of supreme authority in matters of justice by the king's courts, and to suits being brought, on the one hand, from every part of the kingdom before a comparatively small number of judges having their "certain place"[1] at Westminster, and, on the other hand, dealt with in every part of the kingdom by the same judges on their circuits.

It would not be appropriate here to discuss the relative advantages of the English (or, as it should now be called, Anglo-American) and the continental usage. With the continental method it is, or ought to be, easier to correct anomalies and reverse or arrest wrong tendencies before they become inveterate. With ours the law, when once defined by authority on any point, is or ought to be more certain. On the other hand, when

[1] The well-known phrase of Magna Carta, c. 17.

case-law has taken a wrong turn, the correction of it by express legislation, at any rate with our English parliamentary procedure, is both an inconvenient and an uncertain operation.

CHAPTER II

THE SOURCES OF ENGLISH LAW

[Compare Kent's *Commentaries on American Law*, with O. W. Holmes's notes, vol. i. Lects. xx. xxi. xxii.]

THE sources from which the law of England is derived may be distributed under the two great heads of that which is "written" or *enacted*, and that which is "unwritten" or *not enacted*. The following statement is intended to exhibit facts which exist and can be verified apart from any controverted question in the philosophy of law. **Written and unwritten law.**

A. *Enacted*— **Written: original and delegated legislation.**

By *original* legislative authority:

Acts of Parliament.

By *delegated* legislative authority:

Orders in Council, Rules of Court, by-laws and regulations of local governing bodies, railway and other public companies, made in the exercise of powers conferred by Parliament, Statutes of Universities and Colleges, and the like.

By *customary* authority (now of little importance).[1]

It is necessary, in constitutional law, to distinguish *delegated* authority from the kind of authority which, though created by the Imperial Parliament, and in point of strict law revocable or variable by its act alone, is not *delegated* but rather *devolved*. The legislatures of British India and of (at any rate) the self-governing British colonies derive their powers from Acts of Parliament, and those powers are limited in certain ways, but such a legislature is not a mere delegate or agent of the Imperial Parliament. Its powers are plenary within the appointed limits; so long as these are not exceeded, there is no restriction on the manner in which the power may be exercised. A town council cannot delegate the making of by-laws to the town clerk, nor a railway company to the traffic manager; the university could not enact that the terms of a statute should be settled by the vice-chancellor

[1] By-laws of local inferior courts made by virtue of a custom are believed to be the only examples of this class.

and the registrar. But a colonial legislature has plenary powers within the bounds of its own competence, and can, within these bounds, confer delegated or discretionary authority in the same manner as the Imperial Parliament itself. This rule, moreover, applies to the Provincial Legislatures established in Canada by the British North America Act as well as to the Dominion Parliament.[1]

The legislative or quasi-legislative acts of bodies and persons duly exercising authority derived from Parliament have of course the force of law as regards all persons whom they concern. "Every by-law is a law, and as obligatory to all persons bound by it, that is, within its jurisdiction, as any act of parliament, only with this difference, that a by-law is liable to have its validity brought in question, but an act of parliament is not."[2]

B. *Not Enacted*—

Unwritten: judicial and non-judicial exposition.

Declarations and expositions of law are

a. Judicial, namely the decisions of the superior courts of justice and the reasons assigned for them.

[1] India: *R.* v. *Burah* (1878), 3 App. Ca. 889, 904. Ontario: *Hodge* v. *R.* (1883), 9 App. Ca. 117, 132. New South Wales: *Powell* v. *Apollo Candle Co.* (1885), 10 App. Ca. 282, 289. New Zealand: *Ashbury* v. *Ellis* (1893), A.C. 339.

[2] Holt, C.J., in *City of London* v. *Wood*, 12 Mod. at p. 678.

b. Non-judicial, namely in (i) "books of authority" (a limited and exceptional class): (ii) writings not of authority, but which may help towards the formation of authority.

No general description can be given of what constitutes a "book of authority." It is a matter of judicial custom and professional tradition. We have already seen that being written by a judge does not make a book authoritative. Some books which are highly esteemed, and which it is not improper to cite in argument, are still short of having authority in the professional sense; Blackstone is the leading example. Sir Michael Foster's treatise on *Crown Law*, first published in 1762, only three years before Blackstone's *Commentaries*, is said to be the latest book to which authority in the exact sense can be ascribed.

Official character of written law.

It will be observed that there is a practical difference of some importance between our "written" and "unwritten" materials, depending on the manner in which they are produced. "Written" law, generally speaking, bears a political and official stamp. It is the work of statesmen, members of parliament, public officers, or the executive officers of bodies whose functions are recognised and regulated by the Legislature as being of a public character. Those who undertake the framing either of Bills introduced in Parliament, or of subordinate acts of legislation, municipal by-laws, college statutes and so forth, may and often do seek the assistance of skilled lawyers to express their intentions in proper form; but there is no security that this shall be done. If it is done, there is no security, in the case of Acts of Parliament at any rate, that it may not be undone at the last moment by amateur amendments. The work of legislators may be and ought to be scientific, but it is not essentially so.

Professional character of unwritten law.

"Unwritten law" is the work of trained lawyers, and its character is necessarily professional and scientific. It deals largely in technical terms, "terms of art" as our law-books call them, which laymen are not expected to understand. The "general reader" who should take up at random, for example, a judgment of the Court of Appeal in the current number of the *Law Reports*, or a case from the early part of the century in a volume of the *Revised Reports*, would have no right to expect it to be more intelligible or interesting to him than a modern technical treatise on engineering or chemistry. Doubtless there is no branch of human affairs with which courts of law may not have to deal; and an intelligent layman who tries the supposed *sortes juridicae* may have a fair chance of lighting upon something that concerns his own business, or is connected with some well known piece of history, or is otherwise of obvious public interest; but still it is only a better chance than other kinds of technical works outside his own special knowledge would offer him. A little reflection will show that law could not be systematic on any other conditions. Like other sciences, jurisprudence professes to be intelligible to those who can and will learn it. As in other sciences and arts, there is no short cut that will serve instead of learning and experience.[1]

Relation of unwritten law to custom.

Another distinction to be noted is in the nature of the authority on which "written" and "unwritten" law claim ultimately to rest. In modern experience "written" or enacted law proceeds, immediately, or by derivation, from the express will of the supreme legislative authority. Such exceptions as may now be found are of no practical importance. Law which is not enacted consists

[1] No opinion is expressed here on the distinct question how far, and for what reasons, the training of English lawyers in recent times has been more cumbrous and less efficient than it ought to be.

partly, but by no means wholly nor even chiefly, in the interpretation of public enactments which are in themselves laws binding on all whom they concern, and of private documents which the parties concerned have, under the sanction or allowance of the general law, made a law to themselves. This does not account for the great proportion of our case-law which does not profess to interpret any written law, whether original or derivative, but professes on the contrary to develop and apply principles that have never been committed to any authentic form of words. Such principles are said to be customary, and are described as "general customs, which are the universal rule of the whole kingdom, and form the common law, in its stricter and more usual signification."[1] The courts also recognise and enforce, under certain conditions and limitations, "particular customs or laws which affect only the inhabitants of particular districts."[2] "Leges et consuetudines regni" has been a regular collective name of English law since the latter half of the twelfth century at latest,[3] in other words ever since our law has had any terminology of its own; in the fourteenth century "lex et consuetudo

[1] Blackstone, *Comm.* i. 67. [2] *Ib.* 74.
[3] See the Prologue to Glanvill.

regni nostri" was so well established as meaning the Common Law that it could be seriously argued (though without success) that it was bad pleading to apply the term to law made by a statute.[1] The very name Common Law seems to imply some kind of reference to general usage and acceptance as being the ultimate claim of the law upon the individual citizen's allegiance. In short, the Common Law is a customary law if, in the course of about six centuries, the undoubting belief and uniform language of everybody who had occasion to consider the matter were able to make it so. To this day "coutume" is the nearest equivalent that learned Frenchmen can find for its English name. Within the present century speculative doubts have become current among English writers, not so much whether the Common Law is the custom of England as whether it is possible for any law to be customary. Nothing will be added here to what has already been said in the former part of this book.

The "custom of the realm," and the king's judges.

There is reason to think, as matter of history, that in the critical period when the foundations of

[1] *Y.B.* 19 Ed. II. 624. "Consuetudo regni Angliae" might be used, as by the scribe quoted in Mr. Horwood's Preface to *Y.B.* 32 & 33 Ed. I. p. xxxiii., where we should now say "practice." But the distinction between substantive law and practice is modern.

English law were assured, from the reign of Henry II. to that of Edward I., the king's judges had no small power of determining what customs should prevail and be received as the "custom of the realm," and that they exercised it freely. Thus at the end of the twelfth century primogeniture does not yet appear as the general law of inheritance in England, but only as a custom appropriate to military tenures of land, and occurring indeed in non-military tenures, but there competing, on equal terms at best, with equal division among sons or even the preference of the youngest son. By the end of the thirteenth century we find it established as the general rule, and any other order of succession treated as exceptional. We can hardly resist the inference that it had grown by the steady encouragement of the judges. At the same time there is not much reason to doubt that the judges fairly represented the effective desires and forces of society at large. If there is any doctrine of the medieval Common Law that might be plausibly suspected of being an artificial creation, it is the vehement presumption against agreements and combinations tending to "restraint of trade." But this doctrine occurs in the strongest form, as early as the end of the thirteenth century, in the records of a municipal court in which the king's judges had no part.[1]

The current description of Common Law as the custom of the realm is not, then, to be dismissed as unhistorical. We have only to remember that the king's judges undertook, from an early time, to know better than the men of any particular city or county what the custom of the realm was. Indeed it is plain that local inquiries, in whatever manner made, could inform them only of local usage; and that, so far as general usage really did exist or tend to exist, the king's judges and officers were the only persons who had sufficient opportunities of knowing it; for judicial circuits and personal attendance on the king in his constant journeys made them familiar, in the regular course of their duties, with all parts of the country. More knowledge of England as a whole must have been collected at the king's court than could have been found anywhere else. Being thus taken charge of from its birth by a strong centralised power, and developed under the hands of trained professional judges and advocates, the Common

[1] *Leet Jurisdiction in Norwich* (Selden Society), 1892, p. 52, A.D. 1299-1300: "De omnibus candelariis pro quadam convencione inter eos facta, videlicet quod nullus eorum venderet libram candele minus quam alter."

Law rapidly became a specialised branch of learning worked out by rule, "scientific" law as the Continental writers say. Much of the usage which determined its form was, by the nature of the case, professional and official usage. The methods and practice of the Anglo-Norman chancery could not have much to do with English custom in any popular sense. But the "lex et consuetudo regni nostri" is still there as a whole, and resting on the same foundation, whatever may be the proportions of lay and learned, popular and official elements in any given part of it.

Origin of equity jurisdiction in England.

The body of rules called Equity, and administered formerly by the Court of Chancery, and one or two local courts in privileged jurisdictions, to the exclusion of the king's ordinary courts at Westminster, is no longer a separate system. As matter of convenience, however, it is still chiefly though not exclusively administered in the Chancery Division of the High Court of Justice, and studied by a section of the Bar who make it their special business. And it still presents, as much as ever, a distinct historical problem, one might almost say an unique one. As matter of history no one has ever ascribed the origin of English Equity to either legislation or custom. It is derived from the king's ancient power of doing justice at his discretion, and by special means in cases where the ordinary means of justice failed, a power admitted from very ancient times down to the seventeenth century. This power is what Maine has called "a supplementary or residuary jurisdiction in the king."[1] Lambarde, more than two centuries earlier, described it as the king's "own regal, absolute, and extraordinary pre-eminence of jurisdiction in civil causes," committed by the king to his Chancellor.[2] In course of time it became well understood in what kinds of cases the king, or rather his Chancellor and other learned persons about the Chancellor, would think the remedies of the Common Law inadequate. Relief in the Chancery ceased to be a privilege or bounty of royal grace, and became the right of the subject. When the benefit of the king's equity was once a matter of right, it was inevitable that the rules of equity should become as methodical as any other part of the law. Blackstone could already say with truth that "the

[1] *Early Law and Custom*, p. 164.

[2] *Archeion*, p. 63, ed. 1635. What Lambarde calls "the true moderation of jurisdiction absolute" is discussed by him in later chapters. His opinion is, briefly, that the King in Council may not contravene the Common Law, but may supplement it.

system of our courts of equity is a laboured connected system, governed by established rules and bound down by precedents."[1] Much fuller development in the same direction took place in the generations following Blackstone. Our equity jurisprudence, to use the accustomed phrase, has been formed altogether by the work of learned persons having a great deal of real power at their disposal, and consciously using that power to produce a systematic doctrine. It therefore answers the description of "scientific law" more exactly than any other part of our English legal materials, and perhaps more exactly than any other modern form of "unwritten" law.

We may now find it useful to examine more closely the view taken by English lawyers of the seat and power of the ultimate legislative authority (sovereignty as it is called by our modern publicists) and of the authority and reception of custom.

[1] *Comm.* iii. 432. This tacitly corrects the loose passage in the chapter on the Nature of Laws, i. 62, where however "equity" means judicial discretion if it means anything.

CHAPTER III

SOVEREIGNTY IN ENGLISH LAW

The supremacy of Parliament.

ACCORDING to modern law and practice there is no doubt that Parliament, or to speak more technically, the Queen in Parliament, is sovereign in England, and no other person or body has the attributes of sovereignty. "The one fundamental dogma of English constitutional law is the absolute legislative sovereignty or despotism of the King in Parliament."[1] That is to say, Parliament is the one authority capable of making, declaring, and amending the law of England without reference to any other authority and without any legal limit to its own power. Ever since there has been an English monarchy it has been understood that the king had powers of legislation, and that they ought not to be exercised without advice.[2] From the thirteenth cen-

[1] Dicey on the *Law of the Constitution*, 4th ed. 1893, p. 136.

[2] Leges namque Anglicanas licet non scriptas leges appellari non

tury onwards it was understood, in particular, that new taxes could not be imposed without the consent of Parliament, but other points long remained vague. In later times it has been definitely settled that the only competent advice and consent for all legislative purposes are those of the Lords spiritual and temporal and Commons in Parliament assembled. Later still it has become an undisputed proposition that no bounds can be assigned in point of law to the legislative power exercised with that authority.

The earliest definite statement of the modern doctrine appears to be Sir Thomas Smith's in his *Commonwealth of England*, written as the book itself states,[1] in 1565, and intended mainly for the use of Continental readers.[2] The book was published only in 1583.

"The most high and absolute power of the realm of England consisteth in the Parliament. . . . That which is done by this consent is called firm, stable and *sanctum*, and is taken for law. The Parliament Sir Thomas Smith.

videtur absurdum. . . eas scilicet quas super dubiis in consilio definiendis, procerum quidem consilio et principis accedente auctoritate, constat esse promulgatas.—Glanvill, Prol.

[1] *Ad fin.*

[2] Learned persons resorting to England seem to have used it as a kind of guide-book. See the Elzevir edition of the Latin text, 1641, furnished with an itinerary and other matter to the same purpose.

abrogateth old laws, maketh new, giveth order for things past and for things hereafter to be followed, changeth right and possessions of private men, legitimateth bastards, establisheth forms of religion, altereth weights and measures, giveth form of succession to the crown, defineth of doubtful rights whereof is no law already made, appointeth subsidies, tailes, taxes, and impositions, giveth most free pardons and absolutions, restoreth in blood and name, as the highest court condemeth or absolveth them whom the prince will put to trial. And to be short, all that ever the people of Rome might do either *Centuriatis Comitiis* or *Tributis*, the same may be done by the Parliament of England; which representeth and hath the power of the whole realm, both the head and body. For every Englishman is intended to be there present either in person or by procuration and attorney, of what pre-eminence, state, dignity or quality soever he be, from the prince (be he king or queen) to the lowest person of England. And the consent of the Parliament is taken to be every man's consent." [1]

Sixteenth century theories.

Here we have the first exposition by any English writer, if not by any European one, of the notion of sovereignty in its modern amplitude. Almost simul-

[1] T. Smith, *Commonwealth of England*, bk. ii. ch. ii.

taneously Bodin, writing in France, defined "maiestas" to the same effect, and argued, as Hobbes did afterwards, that in England sovereignty belonged to the king alone. It may well be supposed that Sir Thomas Smith, while he was employed as ambassador to the French court, had Bodin's work in some way communicated to him, although it was not actually published before 1577, in which year Smith died. Apparently Sir Thomas Smith was anxious both to make it clear to Frenchmen that the king of England was not absolute, and to ascribe to Parliament at least as much authority as any Frenchman could ascribe to the king of France. It must be remembered that Sir Thomas Smith, who was the first Regius Professor of Civil Law at Cambridge, was not a common lawyer but a civilian. He was familiar with the Roman adage, *Quod principi placuit legis habet vigorem*, and was determined, it seems, to show his Continental colleagues in Roman learning that we had as good a sovereign as any of theirs. He saw the importance of the point as clearly as Hobbes did seventy years later, and, using his insight with greater political wisdom, boldly put, not the king alone, but the King in Parliament, in the place of the Roman Emperor. In this he was somewhat before his age. His view is amply justified by all modern constitutional writers. Blackstone expressly declares that the sovereignty of the British constitution is lodged in Parliament,[1] and that it is "the place where that absolute despotic power which must in all governments reside somewhere, is intrusted by the constitution of these kingdoms"; after which he almost repeats Sir Thomas Smith's language.[2] But in Sir Thomas Smith's own time the sages of the Common Law would hardly have agreed with him. Their opinion seems to have been that not only the king was subject to the law, but the law was in some way above Parliament. Some fundamental principles of law and justice, never defined but generically described as "common right," were sacred against the legislature, and if Parliament were to transgress them it would be the right and the duty of the judges to pay no attention to such enactments.

Blackstone.

Coke enounced this opinion with his usual vehemence and even more than his usual inaccuracy or disingenuousness in reading his own particular opinion into the authorities on which he professed to rely.[3] He found, as will appear below, nominal

[1] *Comm.* i. 51. [2] *Ib.* 160, 161.

[3] *Bonham's* Ca. 8 Rep. 118 *a*: "It appears in our books that in many cases the common law will control acts of parliament and sometimes adjudge them to be utterly void; for when an act of

followers down to the eighteenth century. Blackstone, however, while in one place he makes a nominal concession to the "law of nature," uses quite other language when he comes to the practical side of English institutions. He denies in particular what he has seemed to admit in general; he will hear nothing of any human authority being empowered to control the Parliament of Great Britain, and explains away the sayings of his predecessors as meaning only that Acts of Parliament are to be construed in a reasonable sense if possible. It is worth while to compare the passages.

"It [the law of nature] is binding over all the globe, in all countries, and at all times; no human laws are of any validity, if contrary to this."[1]

"Acts of parliament that are impossible to be performed are of no validity; and if there arise out of them collaterally any absurd consequences, mani-

parliament is against common right and reason, or repugnant, or impossible to be performed, the common law will control it and adjudge such act to be void; and therefore in 8 Ed. III. 30. . . . Herle saith, some statutes *are made against law and right*, which those who made them perceiving, would not put them in execution." The italicised words are a mere gloss of Coke's own. What Herle did say, as reported, is "Ils sont ascuns statutes faitz que celuy mesme qui les fist ne les voleit pas mettre en fait." Plenty of modern statutes have been inoperative in practice, not because the common law controlled them, but because they were in fact unworkable.

[1] *Comm.* i. 41.

festly contradictory to common reason, they are, with regard to those collateral consequences, void. I lay down the rule with these restrictions; though I know it is generally laid down more largely, that acts of parliament contrary to reason are void. But if the parliament will positively enact a thing to be done which is unreasonable, I know of no power in the ordinary forms of the constitution that is vested with authority to control it: and the examples usually alleged in support of this sense of the rule do none of them prove that where the main object of a statute is unreasonable the judges are at liberty to reject it; for that were to set the judicial power above that of the legislature, which would be subversive of all government."[1]

Modern doctrine.

"True it is that what the parliament doth, no authority upon earth can undo."[2] No case is known, in fact, in which an English court of justice has openly taken on itself to overrule or disregard the plain meaning of an Act of Parliament. The example given for illustration's sake is that an Act making a man judge in his own cause would be void. Thus Holt said: "If an Act of Parliament should ordain that the same person should be party and judge, or, which is the same thing, judge in his

[1] *Comm.* i. 91. [2] *Ib.* i. 161.

own cause, it would be a void Act of Parliament; for it is impossible that one should be judge and party, for the judge is to determine between party and party, or between the government and the party; and an Act of Parliament can do no wrong, though it may do several things that look pretty odd."[1] But this opinion has never been acted upon; and indeed the example is not wholly fortunate, for the settled rule of law is that, although a judge had better not, if it can be avoided, take part in the decision of a case in which he has any personal interest, yet he not only may but must do so if the case cannot be heard otherwise.[2] Nowadays the objection of personal interest in the judge commonly presents itself in the form of the judge being a shareholder (for his own behoof or as trustee) in some railway or other public company whose matters are before him; and it is also commonly waived by the parties.[3]

Acts of Parliament not judicially disputable.

It is now quite well understood that the judges will not discuss the validity of an Act of Parliament.

[1] *City of London* v. *Wood*, 12 Mod. at p. 687.

[2] For a curious early illustration, too long for the text, see the note at the end of this chapter, p. 261.

[3] For a reported example see *Reedie* v. *L. & N.W.R. Co.* (1849), 4 Ex. 244, 20 L.J. Ex. 65, where Parke, B. stated that, being interested in the defendant company, he took part in the case only at the request of counsel on both sides.

They will not even entertain allegations that a private Act was obtained by fraud or improper practices. If Parliament has been deceived, the remedy is with Parliament alone. Within our own time the late Mr. Justice Willes, a great master of the Common Law, and always ready on fitting occasions to maintain the dignity of the law and its officers, laid this down in the plainest terms. An attempt had been made to found an argument on the suggestion that a local railway company's Acts had been obtained, in effect, by a fraud on Parliament.

"It is further urged," said Willes, J., "that the company is a mere nonentity, and there never were any shares or shareholders. That resolves itself into this, that Parliament was induced by fraudulent recitals to pass the Act which formed the company. I would observe, as to these Acts of Parliament, that they are the law of this land; and we do not sit here as a court of appeal from Parliament. It was once said—I think in Hobart[1]—that, if an Act of Parliament were to create a man judge in his own case, the Court might disregard it. That dictum,

[1] In *Day v. Savadge*, Hob. 87; "Even an Act of Parliament made against natural equity, as, to make a man judge in his own case, is void in itself; for, jura naturæ sunt immutabilia, and they are leges legum."

however, stands as a warning, rather than an authority to be followed. We sit here as servants of the Queen and the legislature. Are we to act as regents over what is done by parliament with the consent of the Queen, lords and commons? I deny that any such authority exists. If an Act of Parliament has been obtained improperly, it is for the legislature to correct it by repealing it: but, so long as it exists as law, the Courts are bound to obey it. The proceedings here are judicial, not autocratic, which they would be if we could make laws instead of administering them."[1]

Distinction of legal sovereignty from ultimate political power.

The sovereignty of Parliament being undisputed, we have to bear in mind exactly what we understand by it for an English lawyer's purposes. No power less than the Queen in Parliament is sovereign, for that is the only power which can issue supreme and uncontrolled legal commands. Parliament as a whole, and Parliament alone, can make and alter the law of the land without reference to any other authority. Moreover, we are not concerned, as students of the sources of English law in general, with the manner in which the action of the supreme legislature is determined. As matter of form, this

[1] *Lee* v. *Bude and Torrington Ry. Co.* (1871), L.R. 6 C.P. at p. 582.

belongs to the special study of the English constitution and of the law and practice of Parliament. As matter of substance, the consideration of political power, of its practical seat and ultimate sources, would take us out of the field of jurisprudence proper and into that of politics and constitutional history. It is now generally recognised that the majority of the House of Commons has and exercises, for all substantial intents, political supremacy in these kingdoms. It cannot directly govern at all; it cannot legislate without the concurrence of the House of Lords and the Crown. The Crown, however, can act only on the advice of Ministers, and the Ministers of the Crown are chosen from the party which commands a majority in the House of Commons. That majority, so long as it holds together, can cause its will to be observed, on the whole, in every department of government. Or, to put the same thing in a negative form which is perhaps more accurate, it is not possible for the Government of the United Kingdom to be carried on by any lawful means in continuous opposition to the majority of the House of Commons. But this does not touch the doctrine of legal sovereignty. The power which can ultimately determine the bent of legislation, or control the execution of existing laws, but cannot itself legislate, is not a legal but a political power. Now the majority of the House of Commons, as we said, does not govern or legislate. The House of Commons itself has no power whatever of issuing any direct legal commands except so far as it can do so for the purpose of regulating its own procedure and discipline, and enforcing its own privileges. It may practically make a statute inoperative by refusing to vote the supplies necessary for putting the statute in execution (a thing which has been known to happen), but it cannot alter one letter of the text. This is not what we understand by sovereignty in the legal sense.

It has been said by one or two modern writers that the electors who return members to the House of Commons are sovereign. This involves a still greater confusion of thought than attributing sovereignty to the House of Commons when elected. The persons chosen by the voters at a general election will certainly form that part of the legislature in which the controlling political power resides. But that, as we have seen, does not make them sovereign, much less does it make the electors sovereign. In fact the electors are not legislators or anything like legislators. They have not the power of issuing any legal commands at all.

An identical resolution passed by the electors of every constituency in England, or a large majority of the constituencies, at the time of a general election or at any other time, might be a very notable political event. But it would certainly have no legal force whatever. It would create no kind of legal authority, justification or excuse, and no court of justice would be entitled (much less bound) to pay any attention to it. As Cornewall Lewis long ago rightly said, "The right of voting for the election of one who is to possess a share of the sovereignty is itself no more a share of the sovereignty than the right of publishing a political treatise or a political newspaper." [1]

Cases of complex or divided sovereignty

Although the whole theory of Sovereignty is modern, and in fact could not have been definitely held or expressed before the principal states of modern Europe had acquired a strong and consolidated government, writers on the philosophy of law and politics have readily fallen into the way of assuming that civilised government cannot exist, or can exist only in an imperfect manner, unless there is some definite body in the State to which sovereignty can be attributed. Thus Blackstone [2] says:

[1] *Remarks on the Use and Abuse of some Political Terms*, Lond. 1832, p. 43.

[2] *Comm.* i. 49.

However they [existing forms of government] began, or by what right soever they subsist, there is and must be in all of them a supreme, irresistible, absolute, uncontrolled authority, in which the *jura summa imperii* or the rights of sovereignty reside.

Blackstone's language is well enough suited to the facts that can be observed in the longitude of Oxford or of Paris, and it probably did not occur to him to look much farther. Even in Blackstone's time, however, there might have been some trouble in discovering the *jura summa imperii* in the constitution of the Holy Roman Empire, which was then living in a decrepit old age, but living still. In our own time, if we extend our view eastward to Bern, or as far west as Washington or Ottawa, we may find reason to think that Blackstone laid down the supposed necessity of an absolute uncontrolled authority in terms altogether too peremptory and universal. It would not be appropriate here to enter on the problems, whether legal or political, that are raised by the institutions of federal governments like those of the United States and Switzerland, and in a less complicated degree by those of countries where, as in the Netherlands, or an individual American State within the Union, such as the Commonwealth of Massachusetts or the State of Illinois, the constitution is in fact defined by a fundamental written instrument, and the terms of that instrument cannot be altered by the process of ordinary legislation. In all such cases the ordinary legislative body is in a position much like that of the legislature in a self-governing British colony. We can hardly say that it is in no sense sovereign, for within the bounds of its competence it knows no human superior. But since its competence has assigned and known bounds, we cannot attribute sovereignty to it in the same sense in which sovereignty is attributed to the British Parliament. Where there is a *rigid* constitution, to use the convenient term introduced by Mr. Bryce and Mr. Dicey,[1] there cannot be any one body in permanent existence or habitual activity which possesses unlimited sovereignty. The nearest approach to Parliamentary sovereignty as we have it in England must be sought, in every such case, wherever the ultimate power of altering the written constitution is placed by the constitution itself. In the United States, for example, this amending

[1] A. V. Dicey, *The Law of the Constitution.* Mr. Dicey is, I believe, the first writer who has clearly pointed out that the vital difference is not between federal and centralised governments. It is true that a federal constitution must be rigid, or it will not be truly federal. But a non-federal state may equally well have a rigid constitution, though it need not; and many, probably the majority, have.

power is exerciseable only with the consent of three-fourths of the States expressed either by their legislatures or in special conventions, and, moreover, no State can be deprived of its equal suffrage in the Senate without its own consent.[1] The English doctrine of absolute sovereignty is not capable of being usefully applied to constitutions of this type. In fact it is a generalisation from the "omnipotence" of the British Parliament, an attribute which has been the offspring of our peculiar history, and may quite possibly suffer some considerable change within times not far distant. Such a constitution as that of the United States or of Switzerland may be said to give a definite meaning to the sovereignty of the people, as opposed to the power or caprice of transitory majorities.

Note to p. 253

A case on the privileges of the Chancellor of Oxford is reported at considerable length in the Year Book of 8 Hen. VI., p. 18. The question was whether a certain charter of Richard II. purported to empower the Chancellor to act as judge in cases where he was himself a party, and if it did, whether such a grant was good. At p. 20, Rolf, of counsel for the Chancellor, is reported to have said :—

"Jeo vous dirai un fable [in medieval usage 'fable' is merely 'story,' whether believed by the speaker to be

[1] *Const. of U. S.*, Art. v.

true or false]: En ascun temps fuit un Pape, & avoit fait un grand offence, & le cardinals vindrent a luy & disoyent a luy, Peccasti, & il dit, Judica [*sic*] me: & ils disoyent, non possumus, quia caput es Ecclesiae, judica te ipsum: Et l'Apostol' [*apostolicus*, a common synonym for the Pope] dit, Judico me cremari: & fuit combustus: & en cest cas il fuit son juge demesne, & apres fuit un Sainct: & issint n'est pas inconvenient que un home soit [son] juge demesne," etc.

How this tale came into England I know not. The legend of a Pope having deposed himself was, however, current in the Middle Ages. It first appears in the apocryphal acts of the Council of Sinuessa, where Marcellinus is said to have abdicated or deposed himself for the sin of idolatry (see Döllinger, *Die Papstfabeln des Mittelalters*, p. 48). That story was re-told in an elaborate form by Bonitho, an Italian writer of the eleventh century, and the same Bonitho used it, with only slight variations of language, to describe the fact, in itself undoubted, of Gregory VI.'s deposition for simony at the synod of Sutri, A.D. 1046. No other chronicler confirms the alleged circumstances, and Bonitho seems to have introduced them from the older legend for the purpose of supporting the doctrine that the Pope is not subject to any earthly jurisdiction. According to all other witnesses, Gregory VI. was in fact deposed by the Emperor: see Jaffé in *Monumenta Gregoriana, Bibl. Rer. Germ.* ii. 599. But one or two modern writers seem to think Bonitho's story had some foundation in fact: Baxmann, *Die Politik der Päpste*, ii. 206.

CHAPTER IV

CUSTOM IN ENGLISH LAW

Custom in the special sense.

WE have already seen (p. 239) that "leges et consuetudines regni" was an accepted name for the Common Law as a whole from an early time.[1] In a more limited sense, in which we more usually meet with it in modern books, custom signifies an addition or exception to the general law of the land, established by allowed usage within certain local bounds. The allowance of such special customs is subject to conditions which, according to Sir John Davis's report, were carefully defined early in the seventeenth century by the king's judges in Ireland, when it was decided that "Tanistry," the Irish custom of inheritance, had been abrogated by the introduction of English law. The statement is not strictly of authority, but it has been commonly

[1] Cp. Mr. F. A. Greer's article on "Custom in the Common Law," *Law Quart. Rev.* ix. 153.

quoted in England as a correct exposition of the Common Law.

> Custom, as understood in law, is usage which hath obtained the force of law, and is in truth a binding law for the particular place, persons and things concerned. Such custom cannot be established by grant of the king nor by Act of Parliament, but is *ius non scriptum* and made solely by the people of the place where the custom is received. For where people find a certain act good and beneficial, and apt and suitable to their disposition, they put the same in practice from time to time, and so by repetition of such acts a custom is made, and being used from time whereof memory runs not, obtains the force of law. . . . In short, custom is a reasonable act, iterated, multiplied and continued by the people from time whereof memory runs not.[1] .

Conditions of validity.

The general conditions required for the validity of a local custom are the following:—

1. The custom must be reasonable, that is, it must not be repugnant to any fundamental principle of justice or law. A custom is void which purports to enable an officer of a corporation to give a conclusive certificate in a matter in which the corporation is interested.[2] Customary rights exerciseable over land must be in some way limited so that they cannot be used to the total exhaustion or destruction of the land in point of value.

2. The custom must have a reasonable com-

[1] Sir J. Davis, 31, 32; cp. Blackstone, *Comm.* i. 74, 77.

[2] *Day* v. *Savadge*, Hob. 85.

mencement. This means that it must be capable of being referred to a possible legal origin.

3. It must be certain. For if it could not be reduced to certainty, there would not be any binding rule.

4. It must be ancient. This condition does not seem wholly consistent with the doctrine that custom is made by popular consent; for if so, why should not new rules be made for new circumstances by general consent expressed in habitual action? The historical explanation is that the commencement of "legal memory" was left standing at a fixed date by mere accident or inertia.[1] But perhaps the matter is of no considerable importance in practice; for the truth is that in modern times there is a demand for express regulation as soon as there is any decided bent of opinion. Except in matters outside the scope of positive law, the formation of custom belongs to an archaic stage of legal history.

5. The usage which establishes a custom must be continuous, that is, free from interruption by acts inconsistent with the right claimed by force of the custom; and it must be exercised as of right, that is, the custom must be regarded by the persons concerned as a binding rule and not a matter of

[1] Blackstone, *Comm.* ii. 31, and Christian's note.

individual choice. Continental writers express this requisite by the term *opinio necessitatis.*[1]

Examples of ancient custom.

True ancient customary law of this kind is to be found in local customs of inheritance and customary tenures; also some local jurisdictions had singular privileges and incidents even in relatively modern times. Down to the middle of the seventeenth century the men of Halifax had a customary jurisdiction extending to capital felonies, and including the execution of the sentence by means of a "primitive guillotine." The procedure dated in substance from a time before the institution of the petty jury.[2] Perhaps the only customary judicial privileges of any importance that still survive are those of the City of London. Many boroughs have peculiar local customs as to the tenure and conveyance of land within the borough, and sometimes these diverge very widely from the rules of the Common Law.[3]

Local customs of cultivation such as are associated

[1] Blackstone, i. 78, adds that there cannot be two inconsistent customs in the same matter: which seems superfluous in principle. It is really a point of pleading only. See 9 Co. Rep. 58*b*: the defendant must expressly traverse the plaintiff's claim and not merely allege a right in himself inconsistent with it.

[2] See Sir James Stephen's account of this in his *History of the Criminal Law of England*, i. 265.

[3] *Busher* v. *Thompson* (1846), 4 C.B. 16 L.J. C.P. 57, where the Court did not decide on the validity of the custom.

with the term "Lammas land" are also typical examples of this kind. There is every reason to believe that in many cases they are really of high antiquity. Customs of this class, however, have in many modern cases had effect given to them, not as true local laws, but as having been tacitly adopted as terms or conditions of an agreement. This will be further mentioned below.

The importance of local customs is steadily diminishing in modern practice, except so far as it may be needful to rely on custom in establishing rights of common and the like, which of late years (since about 1865) have been brought into considerable prominence again.

Custom in sense of rules now incorporated in the general law.

Another use of the term "custom" is to denote rules that once formed an exceptional body of law, but have been adopted within historical times as part of the Common Law. Sometimes it is also applied to the reception of a special law, as civil or canon law, within particular jurisdictions; in this connection it either means nothing but the practice of the court exercising such jurisdiction, or it is an euphemistic device to avoid any plain admission of the fact that the Common Law, the law of the king's superior courts, was at one time only one among several systems of law claiming obedience each within its own sphere.[1] In the medieval conception of legal order, custom might just as well be personal as local; it might be the usage of a trade or condition of men as well as of a manor or a city. There was nothing strange in calling even individual habits and predilections by the name of custom.[2] In one case, to use Blackstone's words, "a particular system of customs used only among one set of the king's subjects," namely merchants, and "called the custom of merchants, or *lex mercatoria*,"[3] has been adopted into the general law and become an extremely important part of it.

The law merchant.

At the very time that Blackstone was putting his *Commentaries* into their finished form, in the earliest years of the reign of George III., this process was being accomplished. In the Middle Ages we hear of the Law Merchant as something different from the Common Law, which is administered by special tribunals under the authority of the Chancellor, especially for the benefit of foreign merchants resorting to England.[4] At that time the "custom

[1] Blackstone, *Comm.* i. 79, 80.

[2] See this in Sir T. Malory's *Morte d'Arthur*, *passim*.

[3] *Comm.* i. 75.

[4] "This suit is brought by an alien merchant, who has come here by safe conduct, and he is not bound to sue according to the law of the land for to await the trial by twelve men and other formalities, but he shall sue here [before the King's Council in

of merchants" meant the actual usage of the European commercial world as it then was, which was not too large a world to have pretty uniform rules and understandings. In the seventeenth century we find actions on bills of exchange brought in the king's courts, and the custom of merchants specially pleaded as a kind of personal law binding upon the parties. Thus it came before the ordinary tribunals, but as a thing to be specially proved in every case.[1] Only in the eighteenth century the decisive step was taken of treating the rules of the law merchant as within the knowledge of the judges, like the general law of the land, after they had once been recognised by considered decision. Proof was now neither required nor allowed. "When once solemnly settled, no particular usage shall be admitted to weigh against it," said Lord Mansfield in 1761, declining to make any question, upon evidence of this or that merchant's opinion, of the negotiable

the Star Chamber], and it shall be determined according to the law of nature in the Chancery . . . [and the King's jurisdiction over them is] *secundum legem naturae*, called by some the Law Merchant, which all the world over is an universal law." So Booth, Bishop of Durham and Chancellor, is reported to have said in 1474: Y.B. 13 Ed. IV. 9, pl. 5. (This is the case in which the doctrine of larceny by a bailee "breaking bulk" was introduced.)

[1] The early history of the Law Merchant in England is still far from perfectly known. Mr. John Macdonell's Introduction to Smith's *Mercantile Law*, ed. 1890, gives the best general account.

quality of a bill payable to order and indorsed over without express restriction. "People talk of the custom of merchants," added Sir Michael Foster. "This word Custom is apt to mislead our ideas. The Custom of Merchants, so far as the law regards it, is the Custom of England . . . we should not confound general customs with special local customs."[1] It is interesting to notice that this decision was reported by none other than Blackstone himself.

Not quite a generation later (1787), Justice Buller said in a renowned mercantile case:[2]

> Before that period [*i.e.* about 1750] we find that in courts of law all the evidence in mercantile cases was thrown together; they were left generally to a jury [*i.e.* the rules were treated as matter of usage to be proved by evidence, without distinction of law and fact], and they produced no established principle. From that time we all know the great study has been to find some certain general principles which shall be known to all mankind, not only to rule the particular case then under consideration, but to serve as a guide for the future. Most of us have heard these principles stated, reasoned upon, enlarged, and explained, till we have been lost in admiration at the strength and stretch of the human understanding.

More than a century has passed since these

[1] *Edie* v. *East India Co.* 1 W. Bl. 295.

[2] *Lickbarrow* v. *Mason*, 1 Sm. L.C. 10th ed. at p. 685. The case is given only in an abridged statement in 1 Revised Reports, 425: see the reasons for this course in Mr. Campbell's note at p. 427.

words were spoken, and the development of the law merchant as part of the Common Law of the English-speaking world has continued without ceasing. Being thus embodied in our system of legal precedents, it has inevitably lost something of its closeness of touch with actual mercantile practice. It is as much "scientific" as any other branch of English case-law, and the reasoning of trained lawyers on the settled rules of the law merchant does not always bring out results which appear to men of business to satisfy the requirements of commerce. Yet the ancient character of the law merchant has not wholly disappeared, for evidence of living general usage is still admissible to add new incidents to its contents provided that they do not contradict any rule already received.[1] Thus the whole law of bankers' cheques (which only of late years have become common outside English-speaking countries) is founded on comparatively recent usage.[2] In this department the rule of antiquity has no place.

[1] Cur. per Cockburn, C.J., in Ex. Ch. *Goodwin* v. *Robarts* (1875), L.R. 10 Ex. 337, 346, 352-3. The decision was affirmed by the House of Lords, 1 App. Ca. 476, but this point was not expressly dealt with.

[2] L.R. 10 Ex. 351. Even among English-speaking men of business there are divergences in modern practice. Thus the use of crossed cheques is unknown in the United States.

Usage of the country or of trade read into contracts of parties.

In yet another class of cases we meet with the word "custom." This is where a general and well understood usage in a particular district, or among persons carrying on a particular kind of business, or dealing in a particular market, has been allowed, not indeed to impose a positively binding law, but to affect, and sometimes to affect very materially, the interpretation of contracts made by parties who are presumed to have done their business with tacit reference to such usages. Proof of a "custom of the country" or "custom of trade" is admissible not merely to determine the meaning of expressions used in a special sense, but to add whole new terms to contracts.[1] This perhaps goes near, in some applications of the principle, to evading the conditions required for the establishment of customs in the strict sense; although it seems to have been at one time supposed that those conditions must be satisfied.[2] But the principle, as now understood, is simply to give effect to the intention of the parties, and any indication of a contrary intention will exclude the so-called customary construction of the

[1] See authorities referred to in Anson, *Law of Contracts*, 8th ed. 264, 265.

[2] In the leading case of *Wigglesworth* v. *Dallison*, Doug. 201, 1 Sm. L.C. 10th ed. 528, the usage relied on and upheld by the Court was pleaded as an ancient custom.

terms, or customary additional terms, as the case may be. The present writer has suggested elsewhere that it might be better not to use in this connection the word "custom" or at least to speak by preference of "usage."[1] We have here to do with a canon of interpretation, not with a distinct source of law.

[1] *Principles of Contract*, 6th ed. p. 240. Sir W. Anson (*loc. cit.*) appears purposely to avoid the word "custom."

CHAPTER V

LAW REPORTS

[Cp. "The Reporters arranged and characterised with incidental remarks." By John William Wallace. 4th ed. by F. F. Heard, London, 1882, cited as *Wallace on the Reporters*; Kent's *Commentaries*, Lect. xxi.; and Dr. H. Brunner's "Essay on the Sources of the Law of England" in the Introduction to Holtzendorff's *Encyklopädie der Rechtswissenschaft*, translated by W. Hastie, Edinburgh, 1888. Accounts of the better known reporters may be found under their names in the *National Dictionary of Biography*, and also, as to those who were or afterwards became judges, such as Sir Edward Coke, in Foss's *Biographia Juridica*, London, 1870].

What are reports.

COKE, in the Preface to the Sixth Part of his *Reports*, suggests that Moses was the first reporter. The case of the daughters of Zelophehad, narrated at the beginning of the 27th chapter of the Book of Numbers, is not cited by him in this connection, though he cites it elsewhere [1] to show that "in this point, as almost in all others, the Common Law

[1] *Ratcliff's* Ca. 3 Rep. 40*a*, *b*: "This case seemed of great difficulty to Moses, and therefore, for the deciding of that question, Moses consulted with God."

was grounded on the law of God." That case is stated with great clearness, and expressly as a binding precedent, and moreover it was actually vouched within quite recent years by the Jews of Aden when they petitioned the Government of India to be excluded from the Indian Succession Act.[1] Law reports, however, cannot exist in any proper sense unless and until the habit of relying on decided cases for guidance, and bringing them before the courts in argument, has become well settled. The Roman lawyers, as we have said, relied (with strictly limited exceptions) not on decisions but on opinions. Accordingly the literature of Roman law contains nothing answering to our reports; while a few volumes of collected arguments and opinions like those of Fearne and Hargrave are the nearest analogy we can show to one important class of the materials out of which the Corpus Juris was framed. Reports, again, must be distinguished from the official records of the court itself. These are kept for the purpose of establishing the rights of parties in each particular case, or justifying whatever acts may have to be done in execution of the judgment. They are not intended, in the first line, for the general use or

[1] Mr. (now Sir) C. P. Ilbert in *Law Quart. Rev.* v. 367-68.

instruction of lawyers, and they may or may not indicate on their face the reasons of any decision or the points of law that were in issue. The *Rotuli Curiae Regis* published by the Record Commission in 1835, and the supplemental publication of Rolls of Richard I.'s time, edited by Mr. Maitland,[1] carry us as far back in the records as 1194. These are the earliest consecutive judicial records known to exist anywhere. Narratives of legal proceedings, on the other hand, occur in chronicles as incidents in the general history. Thus the chronicler of a religious house naturally made mention of lawsuits in which the interests of the house, or of the order, were involved. Notices of this kind may be of considerable value: Mr. M. M. Bigelow has collected a goodly number of them in his *Placita Anglo-Normannica.*[2] Still they are not reports as the term has been used by English-speaking lawyers for three centuries or more. Reporting begins when cases are collected of set purpose for professional use and study, and may be said to be full-grown when learned persons make it their business to attend the courts and take notes,

[1] Publications of the Pipe Roll Society for 1891.

[2] *Placita Anglo-Normannica: law cases from William I. to Richard I. preserved in historical records.* By Melville Madison Bigelow, London, 1879.

for that purpose, of such cases as appear to them likely to be useful.

The book now known as Bracton's Note book, and edited by Mr. F. W. Maitland,[1] may perhaps fairly be reckoned a book of reports. If so, we may claim for Bracton, under whose direction and for whose use it was almost certainly compiled, the honour of having been the first of our reporters as well as the first methodical English text-writer. The contents of this book "may be briefly described as transcripts of entries on the judicial rolls of the first twenty-four years of Henry III.,"[2] that is, from A.D. 1218 onwards. Entries of this early period give us, for reasons which are part of the substantive history of the law, much fuller information as to what really happened in court than the more elaborate and formal pleadings of the later common-law system. The only thing which need make us hesitate to call the Note Book a book of reports is the absence of any indication that it was meant to be communicated to the profession in general, or used by Bracton himself otherwise than

Origins in England: Bracton's Note Book.

[1] Bracton's *Note Book*. A collection of cases decided in the King's Courts during the reign of Henry III., annotated by a lawyer of that time, seemingly by Henry of Bratton. Edited by F. W. Maitland. London: Cambridge University Press Warehouse, 1887. 3 vols.

[2] Maitland, *op. cit.* i. 63.

as material for his treatise on the laws of England. It is really half way between reporting and the "common placing" of later times. Much later, and in a roundabout fashion, part of the matter contained in the Note Book passed into English legal literature. Mr. Maitland has shown that the cases of Henry III.'s reign noted in Fitzherbert's *Abridgment*, the main repertory of case-law for sixteenth century lawyers, were derived from the Note Book.[1]

The Year Books.

There is no proof that reports of cases were taken down at the time, for ordinary professional use, before the late years of the thirteenth century. Sir John Davis, in the Preface Dedicatory to his *Reports* (1628), accepted as literal history what Chaucer says of the Serjeant-at-law in the Prologue to the *Canterbury Tales*:

> In termes had he case and domes all,
> That from the time of king Will. were i-fall.

But we must take this as a poetic and humorous exaggeration; for if Chaucer's contemporaries had really possessed anything like a set of reports going back to the twelfth century, it is not very likely that they would have all perished, and most

[1] Bracton's *Note Book*, i. p. 117.

unlikely that we should not have heard of their existence from any other writer.[1] From the year 1292 we have a series of reports of cases decided, partly by Edward I.'s judges on their circuits "in eyre," partly before the Courts at Westminster. By good fortune these reports of Edward I.'s reign remained unprinted until within recent times. They were edited by the late Mr. Horwood with excellent care and skill, and furnished with an English translation. Here, and in Mr. Nichols's edition of the contemporary text-book known as Britton—a model of such work—a student may best make himself familiar with the Anglo-French which was the official language of the Courts down to the fourteenth century, and in which reports were written as late as the close of the seventeenth. The language of Britton and the earlier Year Books is far from being corrupt French or a mere jargon. For quite three centuries after the Norman Conquest French was the current speech of gentlefolk in England. Being transplanted into England from Normandy, and continuing to live as a true French dialect, it developed genuine peculiarities of its own, as Dr. Murray has shown in his Introduction to the Oxford *English Dictionary*, and Mr. Skeat in

[1] Cp. Horwood, Preface to *Year Book*, 30 & 31 Ed. I., p. xvi.

the second volume of his work on English Philology (1891). When Chaucer's Prioress spoke French

After the scole of Stratford atte Bowe

she was not aiming at Continental French; she was naturally using the Anglo-French in which she had been brought up. But the following line:

For French of Paris was to her unknowe

seems to show that the transfer of the English connection with France from Normandy to Aquitaine, and the development of her Continental power and policy under the Plantagents, were in Chaucer's time fast assimilating the French of England to the standard of France. It was old-fashioned and perhaps even slightly ludicrous to speak Anglo-French in good society, and the dialect, condemned to linger in an obscure and artificial life, became ungrammatical and poverty-stricken, and expired in the latest reports of the Restoration period as an ignominious jumble of corrupt French eked out with Latin and English. Before proceeding to any further account of the Year Books, it may be useful to give a specimen of the language in its several stages.

Living Anglo-French, Thirteenth Century, *Y.B.* 20 Ed. I. (A.D. 1292), pp. 192-3.

Anglo French and its degradation.

Howard [arguing]. Sire, par ceu fet ne put yl vocher; par la resone ke al oure qant ce fet fut fet, sy fut le Roy Henri, ke dunke fut, en prison: e desicom le governour e le chef de leis fut en prisone, sy fut la ley en prisone, issi ke a cel oure qant le fet &c. ne aveit yl nule ley; par quey le fet et le feffement est nul en sei.

Sir, he cannot vouch by this deed; for the reason that at the time when this deed was made, King Henry [III.], who then was, was in prison: and inasmuch as the governor and the head of Law [*leis* = *leges*, *sc.* leges Angliae] was in prison, the law itself was in prison: so that at that time when the deed [was made] there was no law: therefore the deed and the feoffment is void in itself (Horwood's Transl.).

This, it will be seen, is pure and grammatical French. The language of the treatise *Le Court de Baron*, probably of the early fourteenth century, published by the Selden Society, is very similar.

Decaying Anglo-French, Sixteenth Century, *Y.B.* 12 Hen. VIII. (A.D. 1520), p. 3. (The question was whether it was a trespass to take "unum canem vocatum a blood-hound.")

Newport and *Newdigate* [arguing]. Semble que toutes fois ou on a ascun tort ou damage, la ley done a luy un remedy, et ceo per voye daccion; donq icy, il y ad fait a moy damage per cet prisel, car coment que cet chien soit chose de plaisir, uncore il est profitable pur hunting, ou pur ma recreacion. Car si j'ay un popingay ou thrush, que chante et refraische mes esprits, ceo est grand confort a moy, et donq si ascun prend ceo de moy, il fait a moy grand tort.

It seems that whenever a man has wrong or damage, the law gives him a remedy, and that by way of action: here then is damage done to me by this taking, for although the dog be an object of [mere] pleasure, yet he is profitable for hunting, or for my amusement. For if I have a popinjay or thrush which doth sing and refresh my spirits, this is great comfort to me, and so if any one take it from me, he doth me great wrong.

Here the French is an artificial version of what was really said in English in Court. The grammar and inflections are degraded (the contracted terminations often prevent one from seeing exactly how far the degradation had gone), and now and then the reporter puts in an English word rather than be at the pains of finding the French equivalent, but still it may be called French of a sort. The French of Plowden's *Reports* (A.D. 1578) is, if anything, better than that of the latest Year Books; Plowden, however, was an exceptionally learned writer. The same may be said of Sir John Davis, in whose reports of Irish cases, dating from the early part of the seventeenth century, the language is not sensibly better or worse. By this time it was a purely conventional written language, and probably no attempt was made to observe any true French pronunciation when there was occasion to read passages from the Year Books or early Statutes in Court, or when arguments were conducted in law-French in the Inns of Court, as they still sometimes were as late as the Restoration.[1]

Degenerate Anglo-French or "law-French." Seventeenth century. Rolle's *Reports*, i. p. 189.

Coke : Ceo n'est d'estre fait nisi request soit fait, come si jeo soie oblige a paier un somme al jour certein sur request ceo n'est ascun dutie devant request (R. [*i.e* reporter]. Quære ceo car Haughton semble a disallower ceo, car il shake son capit [*sic*] al ceo).

Dyer's *Reports*, 188*b*, in the notes added in ed. 1688.

Pas. 37 Eliz. Carnes drew his sword sur le stairs de Court de Requests que est hors de view de ascun des Courts, & la si son indictment ad estre bien drawn il duist aver le punishment come icy.

Richardson, ch. Just. de C. Banc al Assises at Salisbury in Summer 1631. fuit assault per prisoner la condemne pur felony que puis son condemnation ject un Brickbat a le dit Justice que narrowly mist, & pur ceo immediately fuit Indictment drawn per Noy envers le prisoner, & son dexter manus ampute & fix al Gibbet sur que luy mesme immediatement hange in presence de Court.

This, it is needless to point out, is the last stage of corruption. All pretence of conformity to French grammatical forms or of preserving a

[1] Dugd. *Orig. Jurid.* p. 209.

substantially French vocabulary has disappeared. "Patres conscripti took a boat and went to Philippi" is as much Latin as this stuff is French. Such a jargon had nothing left for it but to perish.

The folio Year Books

The Year Books which were printed earlier than those of Edward I. have fared much worse. They were published at various dates from 1561 onwards, but the collected folio edition of 1678-9 has superseded the earlier ones for all purposes except those of the curious bibliographer. It is, however, anything but conformable to the modern standard of editing or satisfactory in use. The size is cumbrous, and the Gothic type, which was retained in law-books, for no sensible reason, long after Roman type was generally adopted, is unpleasant to the eye. Words that were abbreviated in the MSS. are printed in the same fashion, and moreover there is great reason to doubt whether the MSS. were read and reproduced with adequate care either in the matter of abbreviations or otherwise. A new critical edition would be a great help to the historical study of the Common Law, and might quite possibly throw light on principles which have not ceased to be of practical importance, but there does not seem to be any near prospect of it. Meanwhile the reports of several years of Edward III. which were not included in the old editions have been edited by Mr. L. O. Pike in the Record Office Series, in continuation of Mr. Horwood's work. Five volumes (1883-91) have so far been published. Mr. Pike's and Mr. Horwood's labours now make it possible for a student to acquaint himself with the language and style of the Year Books much more readily than he could have done a generation ago. The Year Books are not elementary reading, and are not very often referred to in court nowadays, though oftener than they were fifty or sixty years ago. Many lawyers in good business have never read a word of them, and would barely know how to refer to them. Yet some knowledge of them is needful for every one who wishes to know the law as a scholar and not merely as a practitioner; and those who pay special attention to the law of real property not unfrequently find such knowledge useful in practice. Kent's opinion, expressed less than seventy years ago,[1] that the Year Books "are not worth the labour and expense either of a new edition or a translation" has been refuted, instead

[1] His Preface to the first volume of *Commentaries on American Law* is dated 23rd November 1826.

of being confirmed, by subsequent experience on both sides of the Atlantic.

The reports in the Year Books have every appearance of being notes taken in court and written out without much revision; there is no trace of the judges or officers of the courts having been consulted, or the records inspected,[1] or the spelling of proper names verified. According to a professional tradition which was accepted by Bacon and Plowden, and must in their time have been capable of first-hand verification, the Year Books were the work of official and paid reporters appointed by the Crown; which does not seem inconsistent with the rough quality of the work. It must be remembered that even in the time of Henry VIII. printing does not appear to have been contemplated by the reporters. Bacon endeavoured, and with apparent success for a time, to have the institution of official reporters revived, but next to nothing came of it.[2] We are not told why the system of the Year Books, such as it was, had come to an end.

[1] See *Bro. Ab. Executor*, pl. 22, for an example of the actual judgment in a case being misreported.

[2] *Wallace on the Reporters*, pp. 270-1; cp. the Preface to 1 Douglas. The order made in 1617 for the re-establishment of official reporters may be seen in Rymer's *Foedera*, vol. xvii. p. 27. The reports were to be reviewed by the judges and submitted to the Chancellor.

The earlier private reports.

When unofficial reports were first printed, it was with apologies and professed reluctance. The learned reporter assures us that he took notes in court only for his own use, but his friends must needs borrow and copy them; then he was entreated to publish; and while he was hesitating, he learnt that some bookseller would bring out a piratical and probably corrupt edition if he did not without more loss of time bring out an authentic one. Such is Plowden's story in the Preface to his *Reports*, dated 1578, which served as a model for many others. Doubtless MS. notes of cases were freely handed about among barristers and students, as lecture-notes are to this day in the universities; Coke alludes to this practice when he says in the Preface to the First Part of his own *Reports*—"I like not of those that stuff their studies with wandering and masterless reports." As late as 1765 Sir James Burrow wrote in the Preface to his *Reports*—"I found myself reduced to the necessity of either destroying or publishing these papers (which were originally intended for my own private uses and not for public inspection)." Later still, in 1789, Kirby of Connecticut, the father of American reporters, declared that he "had entered upon this business in a partial manner, for private use." Dyer's *Re-*

ports, first published in 1585, fifteen years before the earliest of Coke's, are the leading example of posthumous collections made up from materials not published by the reporter in his lifetime. Such collections have been of the most various degrees of merit. *Wallace on the Reporters* is the best guide to a critical appreciation of the earlier books of reports.

It may be said in general terms that the work of the Elizabethan reporters exhibits technical merit of a high order, though it cannot be said to be rich in literary skill, and the reporter's private opinions are introduced in a manner and to an extent we should now think unwarranted. Comparison of different reports of the same case may be found to suggest that some reporters, and especially Coke, went very far in editing the resolutions of the court in accordance with their own notions of what was correct. In the seventeenth century the merits of reporting fell off sadly; and the "thin squadron of flying reports" that came forth in the latter part of that century and the earlier years of the eighteenth are with few exceptions of poor quality, and certainly include the worst work of the kind ever done. Lord Holt on one occasion was moved to say of a specially bad example—"See the inconveniences of these scambling reports; they will make us appear to posterity for a parcel of blockheads."[1] While the Year Books are now more used and cited than they were fifty years ago, references in court to the minor reporters of the Commonwealth and Restoration times have become exceedingly rare. From the end of the Year Books to the last quarter of the eighteenth century, that is, for more than two centuries, there was no continuous provision for reports being taken or preserved at all.

Commencement of modern reporting.

Sir James Burrow's *Reports*, dating from 1756 and first published in 1765 (which was also the year of publication of Blackstone's *Commentaries*), may be considered the earliest of the modern type. From that time the Court of King's Bench and its successors have never wanted a reporter; we can go back year by year without a break from the current Queen's Bench Division part of the Law Reports to the first volume of Burrow. In the Court of Common Pleas and in Chancery the succession was established a score of years later. and in the Court of Exchequer (then much below the others in dignity and repute) only many years later still. Burrow had something to say of his

[1] 2 Ld. Raym. 1072.

method of reporting, but the Preface to Douglas's *Reports* (by Sylvester Douglas, afterwards Lord Glenbervie), written in 1782, contains the earliest deliberate discussion of the reporter's office and art with which I am acquainted. During the century which followed the commencement of Sir James Burrow's *Reports*, law reporting was carried on by the private enterprise of publishers and of the barristers who prepared the reports under agreements with them. The reports in each court were a separate publication, and sometimes two rival series were carried on in the same court; and besides these there were legal periodicals which collected reports from all the courts and published them more promptly and cheaply, though in a less elaborate form, than the reports known as "regular" or "authorised."

These epithets do not mean, in English professional usage, that the judges make themselves answerable for the accuracy of the report in detail, or undertake not to dispute its accuracy, but only that the judges are willing to give the reporter such assistance as they can by revising their oral judgments and furnishing copies of their written ones before publication. It was formerly understood that an "authorised" reporter had some sort of moral claim to the exclusive benefit of these privileges in the court to which he was attached,[1] but of late years many of the judges, if not all, have given equal facilities to two or more competing sets of reports, in which case they must all be deemed to be equally authorised. It is hard to say when the practice of judges revising their own reported judgments for publication was first heard of, or became usual. But it seems certain that it had not arisen in 1782, for at that date Douglas, in the Preface to his *Reports*, dwelt in some detail on the precautions he had taken to ensure accuracy, but did not speak of having received or sought any assistance from the judges. Attempts were made in the eighteenth century, as may be read at large in Wallace's book, to establish a kind of judicial scale of merit among published reports, and not only to discountenance but to forbid the citation of sundry books of inferior repute. This kind of censorship was obviously liable to abuse, and has long been obsolete. It is now understood that the only indispensable condition for any report of a decided case being admitted to citation is that it must be vouched for on the face of it by a member

[1] See Sir John Romilly's letter as to the position of Mr. Beavan as authorised reporter in the Rolls Court, published in the Preface to 34 Beav. at p. 8; see also *Law Quart. Rev.* vi. 342, *n.*

of the Bar who was present at the decision. But in case of divergence between different reports of the same judgment, the "authorised" report is taken to represent the deliberate expression of the judge's opinion: for a judge may say things in the course of an argument, and even in judgments delivered without preparation, which he does not wish, on reflection, to be permanently recorded.[1]

Even in the early part of this century it was still not uncommon to refer to private notes remaining in MS. in order to supplement or correct the older reports.[2] Such an occurrence is now most rare, if indeed it is known at all. The records of the court itself, however, always may be and pretty often are referred to when it is material to verify the exact form of a judgment or order which does not appear in terms in the published report. In many American States, and in some British possessions, the judges of superior or appellate courts are required by law to give their judgments

[1] James, V.-C., in *Leather Cloth Co.* v. *Lorsont*, L.R. 9 Eq. at p. 351.

[2] See Lord Eldon's remarks in *Sidney* v. *Miller* (1815) 14 R.R. at p. 250: "He had not been able to find anything amongst his own manuscript cases, but he had been favoured by Mr. Eden with a manuscript note of Lord Northington's of what Lord Hardwicke said in *Brown* v. *Jones*; and which the Lord Chancellor read to the Bar."

in writing. This makes the reporter's office much easier, for orally delivered judgments, however excellent in substance, usually need a considerable amount of editing to bring them into an acceptable written form.

Foundation of the Law Reports.

The reports issued by disconnected private enterprise were, with few exceptions, good enough in substance, and some were very good indeed; but they were costly, bulky, and dilatory, and, as Lord Justice Lindley has said, "the waste of labour, time, and money was prodigious."[1] In 1863 the English Bar took the matter into their own hands, and the labours of a committee appointed to consider what could be done resulted in the establishment of the Council of Law Reporting, a directing body which represents the Inns of Court, and now also the General Council of the Bar.

From 1865 onwards the Law Reports have been carried on by the Council in the interest of the profession as a co-operative and self-supporting enterprise.[2] The example set by the English Law

[1] *Law Quart. Rev.* i. 138. More detail will be found there, and in the late Mr. Daniel's *History and Origin of the Law Reports*, London, 1884, of which the Lord Justice's article was a review.

[2] Most of the existing "authorised" reporters joined the staff of the Law Reports at once; a few of them held out for a year or two, but one may say broadly that the Law Reports absorbed and superseded the old "authorised" reports with remarkable completeness and with all but universal approval. It was no part of the scheme,

Reports was in course of time followed in Ireland, and to a certain extent in British India. Arrangements analogous, in varying degrees, to those of the English "authorised" reports exist in the Federal and State jurisdictions of the United States, and in the larger self-governing British Colonies. In America "the reporters of the Supreme Court of the United States and of most, perhaps of all, the State Courts of last resort, are public officials duly elected or appointed,"[1] and accordingly the reports are constantly described as official, a term which English lawyers have avoided.

Bulk of English and American case-law.

Sir Edward Coke, in the Preface to the Third Part of his *Reports*, estimated the number of volumes of reports then in existence at fifteen. About the beginning of the eighteenth century "a country lawyer who was afterwards advanced to the seat of justice" is said to have complained that "when he was a student he could carry a complete library of books in a wheelbarrow, but that they were so wonderfully increased in a few years that they could not then be drawn in a waggon."[2] Now the

however, to set up an official monopoly of reporting, and other competing series continued and still continue to be published, and to be preferred to the Law Reports, for various reasons, by a certain number of the profession.

[1] Wambaugh, *The Study of Cases*, 2nd. ed. 1894, p. 109.

[2] Pref. to 5 Mod. p. xi.

waggon would be as much out of date as the wheelbarrow. The volumes of reports are something over eighteen hundred if we count English reports alone, and come to two thousand if we add the Irish ones. It is said that the various jurisdictions of the United States have already produced something like double this number. Making a rough allowance for the reports of British India and the English-speaking Colonies, we shall not be far wrong in saying that on the whole there are now in print not far from eight thousand volumes of reported decisions.[1]

[1] Cp. Dillon, *Laws and Jurisprudence of England and America*, Boston, Mass. 1894, p. 265. The statement as to American reports is founded on the estimate there given; but Judge Dillon gives for the English ones a much larger number than I have obtained as the result of an independent verification. It does not appear from what source his figure of 2944 volumes as existing in 1881 was derived. My own round numbers to the end of 1895 are: English "regular" reports from the Year Books, inclusive, 1000 volumes Law Reports and other periodical reports, 625; Crown Cases, Criminal Law Reports, and State Trials, 170; other reports of special classes of cases, about 30: total 1825. Irish reports, 185; Scottish (which belong, however, to a different system of law), 290. This makes for the United Kingdom a total of about 2300. There are some reports of County Court cases, but these ought not to be reckoned, as the decisions of inferior courts may not be quoted as authority. The same may be said of a mass of individual reports of separate cases, collections of celebrated trials, and so forth, which might considerably swell the total if admitted, but of which only a small proportion are properly authenticated reports of authoritative decisions. Inclusion of such publications may perhaps account for the largeness of the estimate adopted by Judge Dillon. The *Revised Reports*, now in their 25th volume, are not counted here, as they are not an addition to the existing reports but a reprint omitting obsolete matter.

Of course no one can pretend to be familiar with more than a small fraction of this enormous literature. In practice a modern lawyer is content to know the current authorities of his own generation and country, and within his own range of work, and a select number of the older decisions on principles of general importance. All the reported English cases likely to be wanted for any ordinary professional purpose at this day might probably be contained in about one hundred and fifty volumes of the size of the Law Reports, and the number which any one man has found it needful or useful to read carefully might possibly fill, at a rough guess, twenty or twenty-five such volumes.

It must not be forgotten that even among the earlier books many cases are reported twice or oftener by different reporters, and in modern times we have series of rival reports which, although they differ more or less in their selection of cases, have a great part of their matter in common. Thus the total substance of reported cases is not quite so huge as it seems. But it is sometimes needful, if there is doubt as to the facts or as to the exact language used by the court, to compare all the known concurrent reports of a case, and therefore it cannot be said of any volume of the reports, even those of inferior authority, that a lawyer may not at some time have to refer to it.

Use of authorities.

The peculiar difficulties of studying Anglo-American law lie, on the whole, not so much in the actual amount of reading that is required (which is probably not greater than in the case of any other learned or literary calling) as in the dispersion of the materials, the rapid accession of new matter and obsolescence of old, and the elaborate apparatus of reference rendered necessary by these conditions, which can itself be used with full effect only after a certain amount of professional training and experience. Every student should accustom himself as soon as possible to the process of ascertaining and verifying, with the help of the various indexes and digests, the authorities available on a given point of law. Lists of the English reports, and the abbreviations by which they are commonly referred to, may be found in Fisher's *Digest* and other works of reference, and in some of the law booksellers' catalogues. A new and, it is believed, a complete or very nearly complete one was issued by the Council of Law Reporting in 1895.[1]

[1] "Tables, Alphabetical and Chronological, of all Reports of Cases decided in England, Scotland, and Ireland . . . with a List of the usual Modes of Citation, compiled under the direction of the Council," by Arthur Cane. London: Wm. Clowes and Sons, Ltd.,

Let the student, above all, remember that in our law text-books are not authorities, with the exception, which in usual practice is seldom material, of the limited number of old books by private writers to which authority in the proper sense has been ascribed. Unverified notes or extracts should never be trusted; neither is it safe to assume that extracts from a case in even the most careful and learned of text-books, though correct so far as they go, and apparently relevant, will suffice for the purpose in hand. The text-writer's purpose may not be the same as yours, and, if it were, the court may not agree with him that the passages he has selected are the only relevant ones. First-hand acquaintance with the authorities themselves is the only safe way.

We shall now proceed to inquire more precisely than we have yet done in what sense decided cases are of authority in our courts, and by what rules or understandings the inconvenience of different authorities being found to be in conflict is provided against or diminished.

1895. This includes not only reports fully published before 1865, but serial reports commenced before that date, and continued afterwards. It does not, however, include the periodical reports of cases in all the courts which have for many years been published in connection with legal newspapers. One cannot be sure that this or any other list accounts for all the obscure minor reports, but it is more than sufficient for all practical purposes.

CHAPTER VI

CASE-LAW AND PRECEDENTS

[Blackstone, *Comm.* i. 69-73; Kent, *Comm.* Lect. xxi.; *The Laws and Jurisprudence of England and America*, by John F. Dillon. Boston, Mass. 1894 (Lects. viii. and x.); *Judicial Precedents: a short Study in Comparative Jurisprudence*, by J. C. Gray, *Harv. Law Rev.* ix. 27; *The Study of Cases*, by Eugene Wambaugh, 2nd ed. Boston, Mass. 1894].

Authority of decisions: its degrees.

As regards the authority of decided cases (which in modern times means, for all practical purposes, reported cases), we have to consider whether they proceed from a superior court of original jurisdiction, or from a court of appeal which is itself subject to a further appeal, or from a court of last resort, that is, a court whose decisions cannot be reviewed by any other tribunal. The decisions of an ordinary superior court are binding on all courts of inferior rank within the same jurisdiction, and, though not absolutely binding on courts of co-ordinate authority nor on that court itself, will be followed in the absence of strong reason to the contrary. The strongest of such possible reasons is disregard, by the decision dissented from, of some still higher authority.

The decisions of a Court of Appeal are binding on all courts of co-ordinate rank with the court below, and generally, according to English practice, on the Appellate Court itself.

As regards a court of last resort, its decisions are certainly binding on all courts of lower rank. Usage differs on the point whether such a court shall treat itself as bound by its own decisions. The House of Lords has gone farthest in this direction; the Supreme Court of the United States, on the other hand, has more than once openly reversed its own previous doctrine; some other tribunals of last resort have not dissented from their own former conclusions except in very special circumstances, but have also not disclaimed the power of doing so.

Few definite statements have been made on the subject by persons speaking with authority, and indeed there has not been much explicit statement of any kind; and, in England at all events, there has been no attempt to regulate the usage of the courts by legislation. What is here said is intended to express the recognised practice and tradition with such approximate exactness as the nature of the case admits of. We shall now illustrate the practice by examples of its judicial declaration or discussion.

Early statements and discussion.

As early as the middle of the thirteenth century Bracton, as we have seen, collected and cited decisions; but there is nothing to warrant us in saying that he regarded them as positively binding on the judges in similar cases arising later. Early in the fourteenth century, however, we find Herle (perhaps the same William de Herle who became a judge in 1320, and Chief Justice of the Common Pleas seven years later) impressing on the court before whom he argues that their decision will be received as authority, and therefore ought to be carefully considered, "for the judgment that you shall now make in this matter will be used hereafter in every *quare non admisit* in England." [1]

This appears to have expressed a view generally admitted, for otherwise we should not find the remark so pointedly reported without any note of dissent from the court, the opposing counsel, or the reporter himself. A century and a half later

[1] *Year Book*, 32 Ed. I. ed. Horwood, p. 33. The question (of which no decision is reported) was whether a plea of three distinct and independent objections to a clerk's eligibility for presentation to a church was allowable or not.

(A.D. 1454) we find Prisot, Chief Justice of the Common Pleas,[1] laying down from the Bench how inconvenient it would be for the court to disregard the judgments of earlier date. The question was on the construction of a statute, and one reason given is that the judges who were nearer to the date of the statute were more likely to understand it rightly; but the general importance of adhering to precedent is also insisted upon. The young apprentices of the law, Prisot says, will give no faith to their books, if points which they find many times laid down in their books are now to be decided the other way.[2] A year later we find Prisot, in a discussion among the judges in the Exchequer Chamber, apparently maintaining the authority of precedent against a majority of his colleagues. The judges, as reported, seem to contradict themselves at different stages of the proceedings, but at all events the question whether the court was free to dissent from a recent decision of its own or not was discussed, in the presence of the Bar, but without hearing any fresh arguments from them, with con-

[1] In *Wallace on the Reporters*, 4th ed. p. 100, the date of this case is erroneously given as 1444, and consequently (it would seem) Prisot, who was appointed in 1449 and was never a puisne judge, is described as Mr. Justice Prisot and stated to have been afterwards promoted.

[2] 33 Hen. VI. 41*a*.

siderable animation, and the reasons given, so far as we can collect them from an evidently imperfect report, are such as might well be given at this day.[1] Fortescue, Chief Justice of the King's Bench, seems to have said at one time that he must acquiesce in a series of decisions which he did not approve, although no judge would in his opinion so decide if the point were new. But on the same page he is stated (whether by the reporter himself, or in an aside of Prisot to counsel, is not clear) to have said that, if there had been such a decision as supposed, he did not believe the point had been adequately argued or considered, and therefore did not feel bound to pay much regard to such a judgment: and this seems to have been his latest opinion, for Prisot's contention was ultimately overruled.[2] Prisot appears to have given the date of the case he relied upon ("il alleg' deins quel an.")

Coke's general statement, in the Preface to the Tenth Part of his *Reports*, that in olden times the serjeants and apprentices of the law "never cited any book, case, or authority in particular" is there-

[1] 34 Hen. VI. 24.

[2] The Year Book report is made almost unintelligible by an erroneous statement of the final result, which is corrected in *Bro. Ab. Executor*, pl. 22, on the authority of the record as vouched by the Court in 23 Hen. VIII. (a year for which there is not any Year Book in print). The law was already settled: see 6 Ed. IV. 1, pl. 1.

fore too wide as it stands in English; the contemporaneous Latin text, however, has "vix unquam," which leaves room for exceptional cases.[1] According to Coke the common form was "it is held" or "it is agreed in our books," "it has been decided in full court," and the like. We must not forget the mechanical difficulty of citing any "book, case, or authority in particular," before the invention of printing; it was not an insuperable difficulty, for some medieval manuscripts are very well indexed; but it was not a trifling one.

Modern usage: as to co-ordinate authority.

Having thus shown that the principles which now guide our courts in following precedents were in existence four centuries and a half ago, we may come at once to the most modern utterances on the subject. Sometimes it has been thought that judges are positively bound to follow decisions of "co-ordinate authority," that is, the decisions of courts of equal rank and exercising the same jurisdiction, unless obviously contrary to higher authority or the weight of previous equal authority. This was the view taken by the late Sir George Jessel in the earlier part of his judicial career.[2]

[1] In the great case of larceny by breaking bulk, in 1473, Y.B. 13 Ed. IV. 9 (translated in Pollock and Wright on *Possession*, pp. 134-137), Brian, C.-J., appears to have quoted particular cases much as we do now.

[2] *Re Harper and G.E.R. Co.* (1875), L.R. 20 Eq. at p. 43.

But some years later, having learnt that the Court of Appeal did not consider a judge of first instance to be so strictly bound, he held himself free to discuss previous decisions of co-ordinate authority on their merits, admitting, however, that "there is perhaps nothing more important in our law than that great respect for the authority of decided cases which is shown by our tribunals," and that the decision of a tribunal of co-ordinate jurisdiction ought to be followed "where it is of respectable age and has been used by lawyers as settling the law."[1] Before the Judicature Acts the different Superior Courts of Common Law, the Queen's Bench, Common Pleas, and Exchequer, treated one another's decisions with respect, but not as authorities precluding discussion.[2] It is by no means clear that they even held themselves positively bound by their own decisions while the judges who had pronounced them were living.[3]

[1] *Re Hallett's Estate* (1879), 13 Ch. D. at p. 712; *Osborne* v. *Rowlett* (1880), *ib.* at p. 779.

[2] Cp. Vaughan 383, where the language is wide. If Vaughan, C.-J., really said that a judge can never be bound to follow an authority with which he personally does not agree, he disregarded the uniform practice of English courts. The language of Brett, M.R., 9 P.D. at p. 98, seems to go a little too far the other way. There is no doubt of the fact that the old Courts in Westminster Hall often took independent lines.

[3] Dallas, C.-J., seems to imply the contrary in *Christie* v. *Lewis* (1821), 2 Brod. & B. 426, 23 R.R. 491.

Correction of manifest error.

Occasionally cases are reported which (whether by some real mistake at the time, or through some omission or misstatement in the report) are, as they stand reported, manifestly contrary to the rules of law as settled and generally understood, or to the uniform tendency of other decisions, the "current of authority" as it is called. Even a court of first instance may disregard obvious aberrations of this kind. It need not and should not throw the duty of correcting them on the Court of Appeal.[1]

Respect for decisions often acted upon.

Where a decision, or still more a series of decisions to the same effect, has been accepted for law and acted upon by many persons, and especially where a rule thus arrived at has become a guide to lawyers and their clients in their dealings with property, the Courts, even Courts of Appeal, are slow to interfere with the rule, and it may perhaps be upheld although modern research has shown that it was originally founded on a mistake; for the reversal of a rule that has been commonly acted upon might well produce an amount of inconvenience greater than any advantage that could be expected from the restoration or establish-

[1] *e.g. Re Klœbe* (1884), 28 Ch. D. at p. 180, where Pearson, J., said of a solitary decision of this kind: "It is unfortunate that the case was ever reported."

ment of a rule more correct in itself. In this sense it is said that "communis error facit ius."[1] Even an erroneous construction of a statute may stand unreversed if it has become, on the plausible authority of a series of decisions, "a law which men follow in their daily dealings."[2] For this reason the constant practice of conveyancers has great weight in support of a decision upon which it is founded, and this even in a court of last resort.[3]

Indeed Lord Eldon said without qualification that in its own subject-matter "the practice of conveyancers amounts to a very considerable authority":[4] and in the same case Lord Redesdale pointed out that, if it were not so, there would be great risk of defeating the intentions of parties who had naturally left it to their skilled advisers to express those intentions in a proper form, and whose advisers had used accustomed forms in the sense regularly attached to them in the profession.[5] In this eminently scientific branch of the profession,

[1] *Stourbridge* v. *Droitwich* (1871), L.R. 6 Q.B. pp. 769, 775.

[2] Jessel, M.R., in *Ex parte Willey* (1883), 23 Ch. Div. at p. 127; and in *Wallis* v. *Smith* (1882), 21 Ch. Div. at pp. 265, 266.

[3] Lord Hatherley in *Bain* v. *Fothergill* (1874), L.R. 7 H.L. pp. 158, 209.

[4] *Smith* v. *Earl Jersey* (1821), 3 Bligh at p. 444, 22 R.R. at p. 43.

[5] 3 Bligh at pp. 461-62, 22 R.R. at pp. 55, 56.

who are as it were the Sappers of the Bar, judicial interpretations of the law, notably the law of real property, are apt to be more freely criticised than elsewhere.

Courts of Appeal.

Decisions of a Court of Appeal (in English practice since 1875, the one Court of Appeal established by the Judicature Acts) are binding on all courts of inferior authority within the same jurisdiction. The Judicial Committee of the Privy Council has declared it to be convenient and desirable for colonial courts to accept the decisions of the English Court of Appeal as authoritative on the construction, not only of English Acts of Parliament which a colonial court may have to apply, but of colonial statutes repeating in terms (as often happens) the provisions of such Acts.[1]

It follows that a Court of Appeal not only can reverse or vary decisions from which an appeal is brought, but can overrule previous decisions of courts below which have not been appealed from, that is, can declare or give it to be understood that they were erroneously decided and are no longer to be followed as authority. The Court of Appeal in England does not hold itself free to depart from its own considered decisions or (according to its

[1] *Trimble* v. *Hill* (1879), 5 App. Cs. 342, 344.

latest utterances)[1] from those of the courts of like authority, namely the Exchequer Chamber and the Court of Appeal in Chancery, which existed before it. Quite lately the court has acted on this view.[2] But it has held itself not bound by the result of a former case in which the judges present were equally divided; for in such a case "there is no authority of the Court as such."[3]

Courts of last resort.

Decisions of an appellate court of last resort are binding on all courts from which an appeal lies to it, and, of course, on all tribunals inferior to them. So far what has been said of a Court of Appeal in general is applicable. But the further question arises whether a court from which there is no appeal shall hold itself free to review its own former decisions or not. It may be said on the

[1] In 1880 a different view was held: "As a rule, this Court ought to treat the decisions of the Court of Appeal in Chancery as binding authorities, but we are at liberty not to do so where there is a sufficient reason for overruling them": *Mills* v. *Jennings*, 13 Ch. Div. 639, 648. In the last resort the House of Lords agreed with the Court of Appeal and overruled the earlier decision; they had not, of course, to decide whether the Court of Appeal was strictly entitled to disregard it or not: *Jennings* v. *Jordan* (1881), 6 App. Ca. 698.

[2] "We cannot overrule *Vint* v. *Padget* (2 De G. & J. 611), for that was the decision of a Court co-ordinate in jurisdiction with ourselves": Lord Herschell, L.C. in *Pledge* v. *Carr* '95, 1 Ch. at p. 52. Cp. *Lavy* v. *London County Council* '95, 2 Q.B. (Lindley, L.-J.).

[3] *The Vera Cruz*, No. 2 (1884), 9 P.D. 96, 98, 101.

one side that even the highest court may err, and that if it cannot amend its own errors upon better information or reasoning they may never be corrected at all; for, legislative methods and procedure being what they are and must be, it is for the most part idle to count on legislation for this purpose. On the other side it is said that certainty in the rules of law by which men have to guide themselves is of greater importance than arriving at the rule which is best in itself or most logically harmonious as part of a system. This seems a good reason why a court of final appeal should not decide without full deliberation, and should be slow to disturb any doctrine it has once laid down or approved, but hardly a sufficient reason why it should disclaim any power of correcting its own errors in case of need. In the absence of an express constitutional provision, or an unbroken tradition accepted as part of the judicial constitution, it is obvious that all such a court can really do is to declare from time to time what it considers the proper usage, and act accordingly in particular cases. The members of the court at a given time cannot make its usage a strict law for those who succeed to their authority hereafter.

At present it seems to be the accepted view

House of Lords deems itself bound by its own decision.

though it is certainly of no great antiquity and rests chiefly on the repeated assertions of one judge, Lord Campbell, that the House of Lords in its judicial capacity should hold itself absolutely bound by its own former decisions. In 1801 Lord Eldon seems to have thought that the House was not so bound, for he said: "A rule of law laid down by the House of Lords cannot be reversed by the Chancellor . . . the rule of law must remain till altered by the House of Lords."[1] But in 1827, speaking in the House of Lords, he said the House was bound by a certain previous decision of its own on a like subject-matter, unless there were special circumstances to take the case in hand out of the governing principle.[2] In 1852 Lord St. Leonards and Lord Campbell differed on the point. Lord St. Leonards gave it as his own opinion, addressing the House, "that although you are bound by your own decisions as much as any court would be bound, so that you could not reverse your own decision in a particular case, yet you are not bound by any rule of law which you may lay down, if upon a subsequent occasion you should find reason to differ from that rule; that is, that this House, like every court of

[1] *Perry* v. *Whitehead*, 6 Vea. at pp. 547-48.
[2] *Fletcher* v. *Sondes*, 1 Bli. N.S. at p. 249.

justice, possesses an inherent power to correct an error into which it may have fallen."[1] Lord Campbell declined, though with expressions of deference, to concur in this: "Because," he said, "according to the impression upon my mind, a decision of this High Court, in point of law, is conclusive upon the House itself, as well as upon all inferior tribunals. I consider it the constitutional mode in which the law is declared, and that after such a judgment has been pronounced it can only be altered by an Act of the Legislature."[2] For otherwise, he argued, the rights of the Queen's subjects would be in a state of uncertainty. In the particular case the House avoided facing the difficulty by treating a previous decision, from which they did in substance depart,[3] as having proceeded on questions of fact. But in 1860 Lord Campbell, having become Chancellor, repeated his opinion in the most positive terms. The statement was at the time gratuitous, nor was it altogether accepted.[4]

[1] *Bright* v. *Hutton*, 3 H.L.C. at p. 388. [2] *Ib.* at pp. 391-92.

[3] Lord Justice Lindley (on the *Law of Companies*, pp. 764, 765) does not scruple to say that in *Bright* v. *Hutton* the House of Lords repudiated that decision, or to describe it as overruled.

[4] *A.-G.* v. *Dean and Canons of Windsor*, 8 H.L.C. at pp. 391-93; Lord Kingsdown, at p. 459, reserved his opinion whenever the question should really arise.

Beamish v. Beamish.

A year later, in a case which Lord Campbell seems to have had present to his mind on the occasion last mentioned, he advised the House, against his own opinion of the history and authorities bearing on the case, that it was bound by the result of a previous appeal in which the decision appealed from was affirmed, or rather stood unreversed, by reason of the House of Lords being then equally divided. In 1843 it had been held, in this not highly convincing manner, that by the old common law of England the presence of a priest was necessary to the civil if not canonical validity of a marriage: an opinion which in 1861 was believed by a majority of the House of Lords and the judges who advised them, and is now believed by most competent scholars, to be without any real historical foundation.[1] When the question came again before the House of Lords, the late Mr. Justice Willes virtually, though not professedly, demonstrated, in a full and most learned opinion, that the supposed difference between the law of England and that of the rest of Western Christendom was imaginary. His reasons convinced Lord Campbell and Lord Wensleydale, but Lord Campbell

[1] *R.* v. *Millis*, 12 Cl. & F. 534; see Mr. Maitland's note in Pollock and Maitland's *Hist. Eng. Law*, ii. 370.

declared himself not at liberty to act on his conviction. He said:

If it were competent to me, I would ask your Lordships to reconsider the doctrine laid down in the *The Queen* v. *Millis*, particularly as the judges who were then consulted complained of being hurried into giving an opinion without due time for deliberation, and the Members of this House who heard the argument, and voted on the question, "That the judgment appealed against be reversed," were equally divided; so that the judgment which decided the marriage by a Presbyterian clergyman of a man and woman, who both belonged to his religious persuasion, who both believed that they were contracting lawful matrimony, who had lived together as husband and wife, and who had procreated children while so living together as husband and wife, to be a nullity, was only pronounced on the technical rule of your Lordships' House, that where, upon a division, the numbers are equal, *semper præsumitur pro negante*.

But it is my duty to say that your Lordships are bound by this decision as much as if it had been pronounced *nemine dissentiente*, and that the rule of law which your Lordships lay down as the ground of your judgment, sitting judicially, as the last and supreme Court of Appeal for this empire, must be taken for law till altered by an Act of Parliament, agreed to by the Commons and the Crown, as well as by your Lordships. The law laid down as your *ratio decidendi*, being clearly binding on all inferior tribunals, and on all the rest of the Queen's subjects, if it were not considered as equally binding upon your Lordships, this House would be arrogating to itself the right of altering the law, and legislating by its own separate authority.

Lord Wensleydale said, more shortly, that, having been one of the judges who advised the

House in *R.* v. *Millis,* he felt great doubts at the time; and he implied that those doubts were now rather increased; but the question must be taken as "finally and irrevocably settled by this House." Accordingly the House proceeded to the further inference (doubtless a necessary one if the original doctrine were right) that the priest required by the law laid down in *R.* v. *Millis* is a third person, and the rule is not satisfied by the intending husband being in priest's orders and performing the marriage ceremony for himself. It may seem startling that questions of legitimacy and property should be treated as irrevocably settled by the result of an equal division of the House of Lords, on argument and information admittedly imperfect with regard to the history of the law; that result, moreover, depending on the accident of the form in which the appeal was presented: but so they were.[1]

Later statements in House of Lords.

Lord Campbell's doctrine has been recognised more than once in later years, though there has not been any such striking occasion for applying it. Thus Lord Wensleydale spoke of the decisions of the House as "no doubt binding upon your lordships and upon all inferior tribunals,"[2] and

[1] *Beamish* v. *Beamish* (1861), 9 H.L.C. 274.

[2] *Mersey Docks Trustees* v. *Gibbs* (1866), L.R. 1 H.L. 93. 125.

Lord Blackburn has said: "When it appears that a case clearly falls within the *ratio decidendi* of the House of Lords, the highest Court of Appeal, I do not think it competent even for this House to say that the *ratio decidendi* was wrong."[1] And Lord Halsbury has spoken of the House as "a tribunal from which there is no appeal and which is bound by its own decisions," and whose previous decisions it is therefore useless to examine on the ground of convenience.[2] It has been perceived, indeed, that however much the House of Lords may declare itself infallible in a juridical sense, it may nevertheless be found that different reported decisions of the House are not easy to reconcile: a tribunal which will not overrule itself *de iure* may sometimes forget its own former reasons and contradict itself *de facto*. This, or something so like it as to appear so to Lord Blackburn, has been known to happen. All that can be said is that decisions of the court of final appeal are not to be treated as conflicting without unavoidable necessity,[3] but if no reasonable

[1] *Houldsworth* v. *City of Glasgow Bank* (1880), 5 App. Ca. 317, 335: to same effect *Harris* v. *G.W.R. Co.* (1876), 1 Q.B.D. at p. 528.

[2] *Darley Main Colliery Co.* v. *Mitchell* (1886), 11 App. Ca. 127, 134.

[3] Lord Selborne in *Caledonian Railway Co.* v. *Walker's Trustees* (1882), 7 App. Ca. at p. 275.

exercise of ingenuity can reconcile them, "the later and more deliberate decision" ought to be followed.[1]

Usage of Judicial Committee.

No other court of last resort has gone quite so far, it is believed, in disclaiming power to correct itself. The Judicial Committee of the Privy Council has held itself free to reconsider a question which it had formerly been compelled to decide *ex parte*, and had decided, on such consideration as was then practicable, against the party who failed to appear. In the result the previous declaration was confirmed, but after full argument, in which the point was treated as open and discussed on its merits. Their lordships, it is true, drew a distinction between cases deciding civil rights and cases involving penal consequences. They said: "In the case of decisions of final Courts of Appeal on questions of law affecting civil rights, especially rights of property, there are strong reasons for holding the decision, as a general rule, to be final as to third parties. The law as to rights of property in this country is to a great extent based upon and formed by such decisions. When once arrived at, these decisions become elements in the composition of the law, and the dealings of mankind are based

[1] Lord Blackburn in *Caledonian Railway Co.* v. *Walker's Trustees* (1882), 7 App. Ca. at p. 302.

upon a reliance on such decisions." But they were careful to avoid any following of Lord Campbell's dogmatism, for they added: "Even as to such decisions it would perhaps be difficult to say that they were, as to third parties, under all circumstances and in all cases absolutely final, but they certainly ought not to be reopened without the very greatest hesitation." [1]

This judgment of the Judicial Committee was delivered by Lord Cairns, then Lord Chancellor. It would seem that he was not prepared to accept Lord Campbell's self-denying ordinance for the House of Lords in its full extent: the Judicial Committee could not, of course, properly express any opinion as to what the House of Lords ought to do in exceptional cases: but the Judicial Committee, advised by Lord Cairns, certainly did act in a different spirit from the House of Lords advised by Lord Campbell. In fact the Judicial Committee had gone very near to overruling itself many years earlier, in 1842, though it was then said that the previous opinion dissented from was "in some degree extrajudicial." [2]

[1] *Ridsdale* v. *Clifton* (1877), 2 P.D. 276, see at pp. 306, 307.

[2] *Kielley* v. *Carson*, 4 Moo. P.C. 63, 91, not following *Beaumont* v. *Barrett*, 1 Moo. P.C. 59. Lord Campbell took part in this decision.

On the other hand the Court for Crown Cases Reserved (which in its own jurisdiction is of last resort) has followed a previous decision of the same Court, though some at least of the judges present were not satisfied with that decision, on the express ground that it was binding.[1]

Of Court for Crown Cases Reserved.

The old Superior Courts of Common Law did not hold themselves absolutely bound by their own previous decisions in certain matters as to which they had a peculiar and ultimate jurisdiction.[2] Indeed it is not quite clear, as already mentioned, that they held themselves so bound in ordinary cases.

The Common Law Courts before 1875.

The Supreme Court of the United States has never held itself bound by its own decisions, and has, in fact, completely reversed a recent previous opinion in at least one celebrated group of cases within recent times.[3] The court was divided, but no member of the dissenting minority suggested that the former decision was not open to review; and it is not an American but a British publicist who has observed that "the reversal by the highest court in the land of its own previous decision may

American Courts of last resort not bound by their own decisions.

[1] *R.* v. *Glyde* (1868), L.R. 1 C.C.R. 139, 144.

[2] *Hadfield's* Ca. (1873), L.R. 8 C.P. 306; see especially per Bovill, C.-J., at p. 313.

[3] *The Legal Tender Cases* (1870), 12 Wallace, 457. And see J. C. Gray in *Harv. Law Rev.* ix. 40.

have tended to unsettle men's reliance on the stability of the law."[1] Whatever may be thought of the action of the court on this particular occasion, it seems clear that a tribunal which, like the Supreme Court of the United States, is not unfrequently called upon to decide great political controversies under judicial forms could not tie itself down to Lord Campbell's rule without risk of inconveniences far graver than any that can result from the opposite course. The like understanding prevails in State Courts, though the reasons for it may not there be so strong. A very learned American writer states it as well known that "the highest courts of the respective States, as well as the Supreme Court of the United States, all consider that they have the power to depart from their former rulings, however inexpedient it may be to exercise it."[2]

Decisions in other common-law jurisdictions not authority.

Decisions on the same or an analogous point, given by a court administering the same or substantially the same law, but in a different jurisdiction, have never been treated as binding by English Courts. They may be treated with respect, in some cases with very great respect, but an English

[1] Bryce, *The American Commonwealth*, 3rd ed. 1893, i. 270.

[2] J. C. Gray, *Harv. Law Rev.* ix. 40.

court is not bound to follow them, and indeed is bound not to follow them if it thinks them incorrect. The decisions of the Judicial Committee on appeal from colonies where the Common Law prevails are the most conspicuous example. At least once the Court of Appeal has dissented from the conclusion of the Judicial Committee on an important point of mercantile law.[1] Such dissent, however, is uncommon, as might be expected; the more usual relation was expressed by Lord Esher in the Court of Appeal in 1878: "Though those decisions are not authorities which bind us, we are always glad to be able to follow them."[2]

The judgments of Irish courts, of the leading American courts, especially the Supreme Court of the United States, and of Scottish courts so far as they deal with principles of general jurisprudence or mercantile law common to the two countries, are held entitled to the same kind of regard.[3] In the

[1] *Leask* v. *Scott* (1877), 2 Q.B.D. pp. 376, 380. So as to decisions on appeal from the old Admiralty Court, see L.R. 6 Q.B. p. 736.

[2] *Acatos* v. *Burns*, 3 Ex. D. pp. 282, 291. Still less, of course, are *dicta* in the Judicial Committee binding, see *A. G.* v. *Jacobs Smith*, '95, 1 Q.B. at p. 483.

[3] See per Bramwell, B., in *Osborn* v. *Gillett*, L.R. 8 Ex. 97; per Cockburn, C.-J., in *Scaramanga* v. *Stamp*, 5 C.P.D. p. 303; per Lord Esher, M.R., in *The Bernina*, 12 P.D. p. 77, and per Lord Herschell in S.C. *nom. Mills* v. *Armstrong* in H.L., 13 App. Ca. 10; as to Scottish decisions *Johnson* v. *Raylton*, 7 Q.B.D. p. 438.

United States, reciprocally, modern English decisions, though nowhere, of course, having positive authority, are constantly cited and discussed; indeed in most States they are oftener cited than the decisions of any other State. And in any one State the decisions of every other State have only what may be called a persuasive as distinct from a binding authority. For all practical purposes, however, it may be said that a rule of general law which has been laid down or approved, to substantially the same effect, in the House of Lords and in the Supreme Court of the United States is the law of the English-speaking world wherever it has not been excluded or varied by express legislation.

Decisions given in Ireland by Lord Redesdale and by Sir Edward Sugden, afterwards Lord St. Leonards and Chancellor of Great Britain, have been treated as positive authority in the English Court of Chancery; but this is an exceptional tribute to the eminence of those particular judges.

Nisi Prius decisions.

Decisions of a judge sitting alone at "Nisi Prius," given by way of direction to the jury, can seldom be founded on full and sufficient argument, and by the nature of the proceedings they have to be arrived at without opportunity for much consideration. Such decisions have therefore never been allowed the same weight as those of courts which are able to deliver considered judgments. Mr. Justice Best said of a ruling of Lord Kenyon's: "No man can entertain a higher respect for the memory of that noble and learned judge than I do; but *Nisi Prius* decisions coming even from him, unless they have been acted upon by succeeding judges sitting in banc, are entitled to very little consideration."[1] The practice of reporting *Nisi Prius* rulings has been abandoned for many years,[2] but many of the older ones have become good authority by subsequent approval, and some of them are the only definite reported authority for points of law now received as not only settled but elementary.

Rationale of the system.

Perhaps the best expressed justification of our system of ascribing positive authority to decided cases is in an opinion given to the House of Lords by Sir James Parke, afterwards Lord Wensleydale.

Our Common Law system consists in the applying to new combinations of circumstances those rules of law which we derive from legal principles and judicial precedents; and for the sake of attaining uniformity, consistency and

[1] *Parton* v. *Williams* (1820), 22 R.R. at p. 422; 3 B. & Ald. at p. 341.

[2] Foster and Finlason's *Reports*, ending in 1867, appear to be the latest series of this kind.

certainty, we must apply those rules, where they are not plainly unreasonable and inconvenient, to all cases which arise; and we are not at liberty to reject them, and to abandon all analogy to them, in those to which they have not yet been judicially applied, because we think that the rules are not as convenient and reasonable as we ourselves could have devised. It appears to me to be of great importance to keep this principle of decision steadily in view, not merely for the determination of the particular case, but for the interests of law as a science.[1]

It would be too much to say that the system of the Common Law secures complete uniformity or consistency. Courts are not only liable to errors of judgment, but may be imperfectly informed. But probably it is more successful in these respects than any other system. No doubt it appears more complex and artificial, but it will be found on examination that in other systems the complications are not so much avoided as concealed or shifted. Either a large undefined discretion must be left to the judge in every case, and uniformity given up even as an ideal, or a mass of judicial or extra-judicial exposition, or both, must accumulate—as has actually happened, for example, in France—and form in course of time a storehouse of conflicting opinions, all capable alike of being cited and used

[1] Per Parke J., *Mirehouse* v. *Rennell* (1833), 1 Cl. & F. pp. 527, 546.

in argument, but none of them authoritative or final. Where the two systems have come into competition, as they have done in the Province of Quebec, the Cape Colony, and other British possessions originally settled under Continental systems of law, the method of ascribing exclusive authority to judicial decisions has invariably, so far as I know, been accepted.

Use of Roman and foreign law.

The more or less authoritative expositions of Roman law, or of any foreign system, by ancient or modern writers, may be cited by way of illustration in courts administering the Common Law, but only on their intrinsic merits, and they can be usefully cited only on questions of principle where there is no apparent reason for the law being different in different countries; and even then it is seldom desirable to rely on them in argument except in the absence of appropriate authority in our own books. There is one, and, so far as I know, only one classical case of the opinion of a Roman lawyer, as embodied in the Digest, being used and avowedly followed by an English Court of Common Law in a purely English litigation. In 1843 the Court of Exchequer Chamber had before it a new and important point on the rights of adjacent landowners to the use of underground waters. There was no

English authority definitely dealing with the point, and the Digest of Justinian was freely cited in argument. The Court thought the English cases, though not decisive, were against the existence of the right claimed by the plaintiff, and added:

> The Roman law forms no rule, binding in itself, upon the subjects of these realms; but, in deciding a case upon principle, where no direct authority can be cited from our books, it affords no small evidence of the soundness of the conclusion at which we have arrived, if it proves to be supported by that law, the fruit of the researches of the most learned men, the collective wisdom of ages, and the groundwork of the municipal law of most of the countries in Europe.[1]

And a fragment of Ulpian vouching and approving an opinion of Marcellus was declared to be "decisive upon the point in favour of the defendants." It is obvious that, as our modern authorities became fuller, cases where it is needful or desirable to recur to the *Corpus Juris* are less and less likely to present themselves. Even in jurisdictions which as matter of history are outside the Common Law, for example in Admiralty cases, the general usage is now not to go beyond our own reported decisions.

Chief Justice Holt's famous exposition of the law of bailments in *Coggs* v. *Bernard*,[2] is not

[1] *Acton* v. *Blundell*, 12 M. & W. pp. 334, 353.
[2] 2 Ld. Raym., 909, 1 Sm. L.C. 10th ed. p. 167.

analogous to the Exchequer Chamber's open citation of the Digest. For, although Holt's material was largely Roman, and he must have known it, he took it not directly from Justinian, but indirectly through Bracton, whom he seems, conformably to the medieval tradition of the king's judges,[1] rather to avoid regarding as a writer having positive authority in the law of England. "This Bracton I have cited is, I confess, an old author; but in this his doctrine is agreeable to reason, and to what the law is in other countries." The Institutes are just referred to by way of illustration.[2]

Foreign law in British possessions.

The administration by English authority of those foreign systems of law which actually prevail in particular British possessions, as does French law in the Province of Quebec and in Mauritius, Roman-Dutch law in the Cape Colony, and (in certain departments) the personal law of Hindus, Mahometans, and others in British India, is altogether a different matter. In those jurisdictions the law of England is itself, properly speaking, a foreign law which can be cited only by way of

[1] "The whole court said that Bracton was never held for an authority in our law."—Fitzh. Abr. *Garde*, pl. 71. This statement must rest on some private tradition: it is not in the Year Book report referred to in the margin of Fitzherbert.

[2] 1 Sm. L.C. 10th ed. at p. 175; similarly at pp. 176, 180.

illustration. But the tendency of both advocates and judges in all jurisdictions is to use and rely on the books with which they are most familiar, even if they be not properly entitled to be treated as having authority in the law discussed and applied by the court. It would seem at first sight rather difficult to import English technical notions into the administration of Hindu or Mahometan law, conducted with professed regard for the native principles and authorities of each system. But experience has shown that, with the best intentions, the difficulty is to avoid doing this. And the tendency is by no means confined to British or English-speaking lawyers. I have seen an opinion of a distinguished French advocate on a case arising in Peru, in which he simply assumed the French Civil Code to be applicable. In fact the Peruvian Code on that head of law was practically a translation of the French Code, but the learned Frenchman did not refer to this at all, nor did he appear to have made any inquiry or verification.

CHAPTER VII

ANCIENT AND MODERN STATUTES

[Reports of the Statute Law Commissioners from 1835. T. E. Holland, *Essays upon the Form of the Law*, London 1870.]

Ancient Acts of Parliament, how framed

The actual procedure of Parliament or of any other legislative assembly is a matter of constitutional law not to be considered in this work. But the place of legislation among the sources of law is very different from what it was in the Middle Ages, and a student may easily be misled if he carries back into medieval history notions derived from the constant and systematic working of our modern legislative machinery. In the Middle Ages legislation was not the primary business of Parliament, and the rule that the king cannot legislate without Parliament was established only by degrees. Early statutes, therefore, are of a mixed character, containing both legislative and administrative provisions. We can hardly separate the declaration of new law from the enforcement of old, the establishment of novel remedies for novel mischiefs or newly detected shortcomings from the king's executive instructions to his officers. The King in his Council is alike ready to make fresh rules, to provide fresh machinery for the better working of existing rules, and to dispense justice in extraordinary cases. Law-making is not yet regarded as a distinct branch of sovereign power, external to the judicial authority, requiring strict and literal obedience, but entitled to nothing more. Hence there is a notable contrast between ancient and modern statutes. "The former," said the Criminal Law Commission of 1835, "often contain little more than the enunciation of a general principle of law, leaving the Courts to work out and establish the provisions necessary for carrying the law into effect, whilst in modern statutes the opposite extreme appears to have been followed; and the enactments are expressed with much useless circumlocution, and are overloaded with minute provisions, details, and repetitions." Again, the wording of the statutes was not finally settled by Parliament itself, but entrusted to a smaller body of the king's learned counsellors and judges. In 1305 Hengham, Chief Justice of the Common Pleas, cut short an argument of counsel on the construction of the second Statute of Westminster with the remark: "None of your glosses on the Statute; we know it better than you, for it was our work."[1] Hengham was Chief Justice of the King's Bench in 1285, when the statute was passed, and would naturally be one of the chief persons consulted. In later times the judges have treated Acts of Parliament as proceeding from a wholly external and unjudicial authority. Coke, in the Prefaces to his *Reports* and elsewhere, gave utterance to the feeling that Acts of Parliament which meddle with the Common Law (that is, with the judicial development of it by the courts) are on the whole likely to do more harm than good. His criticism did not spare even the statutes of Edward I.

Professional jealousy of statute law.

This feeling, which may now be called traditional, is not due merely to blind professional dislike of change. There is real danger of both the principles and the administration of the law being impaired by the well meant adventures of amenders who are not sufficiently informed to understand the difficulties of their task, and who have not the skill needed for its adequate execution. Both the matter and the form of legislation depend on the will of the legislator, and in almost all English-speaking com-

[1] "Ne glosez point le statut; nous lo savoms meuz de vous, qar nous les feimes": *Y. B.* 33-35 Ed. I., ed. Horwood, p. 83.

munities legislative power has been exercised by assemblies which cannot well be learned as a whole, and which may or may not be disposed to take the advice of competent persons as to the workmanship of their productions.

Degeneration of workmanship in and after Tudor period.

In fact the statutes of Edward I., framed, as we have seen, by learned men who treated the resolutions of Parliament as instructions leaving them a discretion as to form, are clear and businesslike. If they are obscure to posterity, it is because the language and matter are no longer familiar, not by reason of bad work. The great statute of "Quia Emptores," which is still embodied in the law not only of England but of most lands settled from England, concludes by defining what are now called the "extent" and the "commencement" of its operation with precision that modern draftsmen have restored only in our own time.[1] Diffuse language and slovenly drafting became the rule in the Tudor period, concurrently with an enormous increase of legislative activity. The Crown had discovered that Parliament could be used as a revolutionary engine of despotic authority under

[1] Et sciendum quod istud statutum locum tenet de terris venditis tenendis in feodo simpliciter tantum, et se extendit ad tempus futurum, et incipiet locum tenere ad festum sancti Andree proximo futurum.

constitutional forms, and it was used without sparing, but also without any method being elaborated. When an enactment of ambitious design and wide application, like the Statute of Uses, was found inadequate for its purposes, the failure, together with the various unintended consequences and complications, was almost entirely left to itself. In this period ordinary legislation was dwarfed to a considerable extent by proceedings which were legislative in form, but in fact political acts of State, such as the series of statutes which carried out the abolition of Papal supremacy and the reconstitution of the Church of England.

In the seventeenth century, too, constitutional questions had the upper hand. From the Stuart reigns we have perhaps half a dozen Acts of Parliament which have left a permanent mark on the ordinary civil law between subject and subject.[1] Thus the formal art of legislation received no consideration and made no progress at all for more than two centuries. Rapid increase in the bulk of legislation is a conspicuous feature of the eighteenth century, but, as in the sixteenth century, the quality of the work becomes worse rather than better as the

[1] The Statutes of Limitation of Actions (James I.) and those of Wards and Liveries, Frauds, and Distributions (Charles II.) are, I believe, the only important ones.

quantity turned out is greater. It is true that in the first half of the eighteenth century there was a good deal of useful amendment of legal procedure, afterwards forgotten just because it had done its business without trouble; but the enlightened judges or chancellors who procured this to be done left posterity to rest on their labours, and no school or tradition of good workmanship was founded. About the end of the last century the only art of the parliamentary draftsman was to pile up as many words as possible, significant and insignificant, on the chance that in their multitude the intention of the enactment might find safety. Perhaps the style and structure of Acts of Parliament were at their very worst in the generation immediately preceding the Reform Act of 1832. The Copyright Act of 1842 is among the latest legacies of the bad old style of drafting, and a more flagrant specimen could not easily be found. Improvement began only when the burden was becoming intolerable.

Bacon's proposals for reform.

Proposals for systematic reform had not been wanting, indeed, from the time when the mischief was first felt. Sir Nicholas Bacon, the father of Francis Bacon, formed a plan of this kind as early as 1557,[1] and his more illustrious son put forward

[1] See the *Report of the Statute Law Commission*, 1835.

in 1616 a carefully considered "Proposition touching the compiling and amendment of the laws of England."[1] Many of his ideas anticipate the work of modern law reformers, and some, though not all, have been more or less carried out in our own time. He desired to have a digest of ancient legal rules (for convenience, not as an authoritative text), and revised editions of the Statutes and the Year Books, omitting obsolete matter. He did not recommend the framing of a new "text law"—what we should now call a code—of the Common Law: "I dare not advise," he said, "to cast the law into a new mould." Coke, no friend of Bacon's, gave a limited approval to the scheme, so far as related to consolidation and amendment of statutes, in the Preface to the Fourth Part of his *Reports*. Nothing was done, however, for more than two centuries afterwards.

The movement whose great monuments in political history are the first Reform Bill and the Municipal Corporations Act at last gave an effectual impulse in this direction also. A series

Modern statute law commissions and revision.

[1] *Letters and Life*, ed. Spedding, vi. 61. An earlier draft of the same project is also preserved, *op. cit.* v. 84. The Aphorisms appended to book viii. of the "De Augmentis" (in *Phil. Works*, vol. i.) have been cited by modern Continental as well as English writers, and contain much that is still of value.

of Commissions considered the consolidation and improvement of the criminal law and of statute law generally during many years from 1834 onwards. The positive results obtained were for a considerable time so scanty as to seem altogether inadequate to the labour expended. Nevertheless we can now see that the labour was not thrown away, for it bore fruit surely, though slowly, in the course of the next generation.[1] The improvements effected within the last fifty years, have not, it is true, yet made the form of English legislation perfect. Over and over again the most competent critics have lamented the want of a final revising hand. Many troubles and blunders would have been saved if Parliament could have entrusted the last touches of draftsmanship to some permanent and impartial expert body. The function of removing obvious blemishes of form is at present not regularly committed to any one, and the House of Lords can exercise it only occasionally and partially. Political difficulties have so far been insuperable, and not only elegance but even clearness of language has

[1] The Reports extend from 1834 to 1845. There was a Board for the Revision of the Statute Law from 1854 to 1859, which made extensive preparations but was prevented (it seems by differences of opinion in details) from completing anything. References to its publications may be found in Professor Holland's *Essays upon the Form of the Law*, p. 117.

often to be knowingly sacrificed to the exigencies of working a Bill through Committee in the House of Commons with as little contentious discussion as possible. With all drawbacks, however, the improvements effected are such as would have seemed impossible to a lawyer of Blackstone's or Eldon's time. Obsolete and merely temporary or otherwise expired enactments are now systematically repealed by Statute Law Revision Acts, and the process has been brought down to Acts of the year 1881. The revised edition of the Statutes which has been made possible by this process, together with the official Index, which is periodically re-issued, and embodies the latest alterations down to its date, enables us to ascertain with comparative ease what legislation is actually in force on any given topic.[1] The Interpretation Act of 1889, which superseded a similar but much less complete and workmanlike statute of 1850 known as "Lord Brougham's Act," has ensured reasonable conciseness and approximate uniformity in the wording at any rate of Acts of Parliament introduced by Ministers and prepared in the Parliamentary Counsel's Office, which has

[1] But the student must not suppose that the Statutes at large have become a superfluous ornament in a library. Reference to repealed and obsolete Acts is often necessary for practical as well as historical purposes.

been raised, chiefly by the work of Lord Thring while he was at its head, to the rank of a distinct and important State department. The chief danger of downright bad drafting is now in private members' amendments.

The Clauses Consolidation system.

In 1845 the provisions usually inserted in special Acts forming public companies, and authorising them to acquire land for their works, were embodied once for all in the Companies Clauses, Lands Clauses, and Railways Clauses Consolidation Acts, "as well for the purpose of avoiding the necessity of repeating such provisions in each of the several Acts relating to such undertakings as for ensuing greater uniformity in the provisions themselves."[1] It is said that in the first seven years after this system came into operation it saved 100,000 folio pages of print. Allowing something for the increasing rate of commercial development in the time that has since elapsed, the saving down to the present date may well be estimated at not less than a million pages. This admirable and beneficent invention, which everybody now takes as a matter of course, was due to Mr. Booth, then the Speaker's Counsel. In our own time the same system has been applied, with slight modification, to the Mutiny

[1] These words are identical in the preamble to each of the Acts.

Act. The Army Act, 1881, stands permanently on the Statute-book, and is continued in force by an annual Act. Vain repetition of the provisions for the government and discipline of the army is thus avoided, while the constitutional control of Parliament is as effectively maintained as ever.

Consolidating and codifying Acts.

Many considerable bodies of statute law have been consolidated at various times, and in some cases the consolidating Acts are really codes to the extent of the subjects dealt with. The first notable example of this process was, I believe, the Merchant Shipping Act of 1854; just forty years later this and the later Acts on the same matters were consolidated in the Merchant Shipping Act, 1894, which fills 292 pages in the Law Reports edition of the Statutes. Other groups of Acts relating to various branches of public law,—Public Health, Inland Revenue, and others,—which formerly, by their intricacy and the number of partial repeals and amendments, presented great difficulties even to experts, have from time to time been brought together in an orderly fashion. More than this, a certain number of well settled portions of our general commercial law have been declared in statutory form, codified in fact, with the general approval of men of business and acquiescence of lawyers. Bills of Exchange and other negotiable instruments were thus dealt with in 1882, Partnership in 1890, the Sale of Goods in 1893. So far these codifying measures have worked quite smoothly and have given rise practically to no litigation; that is to say, the cases decided on their construction have been very few, and of those almost all have been on questions of principle which the Acts had left open because the existing law left them open, and which would equally have called for a decision in a jurisdiction where no such statute existed. Our statutory criminal law remains, in point of form at least, in a relatively backward condition, notwithstanding the laudable endeavours of the late Sir James Stephen and others. Many portions of it, and some of the most important, are unavoidably entangled with controversial matter of several kinds, so that non-contentious amendment seems extremely difficult. Yet the Italians have succeeded, under a system of parliamentary government not widely different in principle from our own, in passing a new and thoroughly revised Penal Code. Here we can only note the fact that England has made no advance on the Criminal Law Consolidation Acts of 1861, which are not codifying Acts because they assume knowledge of a great deal of unwritten law; for example, the definitions of murder, manslaughter, and larceny. Broadly speaking, the administration of our criminal law—what the French call *pénalité*—is now mostly if not wholly reduced to the written form: the substance of it is not.

Lord Westbury's elaborate project for a Digest of the whole law, which seemed to promise great things a generation ago, and came to an end in 1870, need be mentioned here only for the purpose of showing that it has not been overlooked. It not only failed of its immediate purpose, but failed to leave any considerable result, save that two of the gentlemen employed to prepare specimens of the proposed digest converted their work into meritorious and useful text-books of the ordinary type, which went through several editions.[1] To the present writer, at any rate, it seems that the example of the Anglo-Indian Codes[2] has been more practical and fruitful. Codification was forced upon British India by the necessities of Indian Codification.

[1] One of these is *Goddard on Easements*: the Preface to the fourth edition contains an account of the Digest of Law Commission, which is now omitted in the fifth (1896).

[2] Edited by Dr. Whitley Stokes, Oxford, 1887. See his Introduction for a short history of codification in India. See, too, Sir Courtenay Ilbert's articles, "Indian Codification," *Law Quart. Rev.* v. 347; "Sir James Stephen as a Legislator," *ib.* x. 222; and an article of my own on the Life of Sir James Stephen in the *National Review* for August 1895.

government, and the experiment has on the whole been remarkably successful. There is no reason why it should not succeed in England when public education is sufficiently advanced to demand it, and competent English lawyers are set to do the work instead of discussing whether it is possible. For the commercial parts of our unwritten law codification is already accepted in principle, and has been carried into execution in some important branches. The further extension of the process is, in my opinion, no longer doubtful in principle, but only in time and opportunity. But the question involves so much controversial matter, and is so far from elementary, that it cannot properly be pursued in this work. In the United States there is quite as much difference of opinion as here, and the discussion has been complicated by premature and over-ambitious legislation, or attempts at legislation, in some of the States.[1] Meanwhile the improvements in form which are effected in this country are for the most part followed, after no long interval, by substantially identical legislation in the English-speaking colonies. The consideration that statutory consolidation and amendment of the

[1] See Judge John F. Dillon's *Laws and Jurisprudence of England and America*, Lect. ix., for a summary of American facts and opinions.

Common Law in this country are likely to be taken as an example by great part of the English-speaking world is a reason for proceeding with the utmost caution and employing the very best learning and skill that can be secured for the work. It is no reason for leaving a great and beneficial work undone, but rather for keeping it constantly in view, and advancing it as occasion serves.

INDEX

Printed by R. & R. Clark, Limited, *Edinburgh*.

www.ingramcontent.com/pod-product-compliance
Lightning Source LLC
Chambersburg PA
CBHW030915270326
41929CB00008B/711
* 9 7 8 3 3 3 7 3 1 4 8 6 6 *